George Butler

The Change of the Sabbath

George Butler

The Change of the Sabbath

ISBN/EAN: 9783743325418

Manufactured in Europe, USA, Canada, Australia, Japa

Cover: Foto ©ninafisch / pixelio.de

Manufactured and distributed by brebook publishing software (www.brebook.com)

George Butler

The Change of the Sabbath

THE CHANGE OF THE SABBATH:

WAS IT BY

DIVINE OR HUMAN AUTHORITY?

BY GEO. I. BUTLER.

REVIEW AND HERALD PUBLISHING CO.,
BATTLE CREEK, MICH.; CHICAGO, ILL.;
TORONTO, ONTARIO.
1889.

COPYRIGHT, 1889, BY GEO. I. BUTLER.

ALL RIGHTS RESERVED.

PREFACE.

THIS pamphlet has been written with the hope that it may find access to a large number of people who desire information concerning the change of the Sabbath,— a subject which is attracting more attention at the present time than it has for ages. Frequent inquiries concerning the day are being sent to prominent theologians and scholars, and to the leading secular and religious papers, asking for light; and the question is fast becoming a prominent one. Thousands of sermons, in the aggregate, have been preached in recent years upon this subject, nor is the agitation likely to subside. As the public mind is being stirred, there seems to be a demand for more stringent laws, both State and national, in behalf of the popular rest day; and as we are living in an age when libraries are being searched, ruins of ancient cities are being dug up, and everything questioned to find the substratum of truth on every subject, it is certainly appropriate that the scriptural and historical evidences relative to the Sabbath institution should be considered.

The questions are often asked, How was the change from the observance of the seventh to the first day of the week brought about? On what authority does it stand? The following pages will quite fully answer these queries, although the work does not aim to be a thorough exposition of the subject treated. Those in search of such a book are referred to the "History of the Sabbath," issued by the publishers of this pamphlet. The "History of the Sabbath" carefully canvasses the entire ground of sacred and profane history, noticing every point, and answering every question. But as many cannot take the time required to read such an exhaustive treatise, this pamphlet has been prepared, which covers the ground of the change of the Sabbath as briefly as is consistent with a clear discussion of the subject, and gives a concise outline of the steps taken in bringing about the change. It is hoped that this work will prove a fair synopsis of the subject, and answer in a satisfactory manner the question, Who changed the Sabbath?

G. I. B.

CONTENTS.

	PAGE.
CHAPTER I. — The Sabbath a Living Issue	7–10
CHAPTER II. — Origin of the Sabbath	11–15
CHAPTER III. — The Sabbath Previous to the Giving of the Law	15–22
CHAPTER IV. — The Sabbath at Sinai	22–24
CHAPTER V. — What the Fourth Commandment Requires	25–27
CHAPTER VI. — The Sabbath from the Giving of the Law to the Resurrection of Christ	27–34
CHAPTER VII. — From the Resurrection to the Ascension of Christ	34–49
CHAPTER VIII. — Sunday Sacredness	49–60
CHAPTER IX. — Apostolic Times	61–81
CHAPTER X. — The Two Rest Days in Secular History	81–88
CHAPTER XI. — The Day that Was Observed in the First Centuries of the Christian Era	88–99
CHAPTER XII. — Steps by which Sunday Gained Prominence	100–114
CHAPTER XIII. — Other Reasons why Sunday Was Favored	114–120
CHAPTER XIV. — A Law for Resting on Sunday	120–131
CHAPTER XV. — Sunday Down to the Reformation	131–142

CHAPTER XVI. — THE REFORMERS AND THE SABBATH QUESTION 142-151

CHAPTER XVII. — TRACES OF THE SABBATH 151-164

CHAPTER XVIII. — WHAT CATHOLIC AUTHORITIES SAY ABOUT THE CHANGE 165-177

CHAPTER XIX. — TESTIMONY OF PROTESTANTS 177-182

CHAPTER XX. — GENERAL OBSERVATIONS AND CONCLUSIONS 182-203

CHAPTER XXI. — SUMMARY OF FACTS ABOUT THE SEVENTH DAY 204-213

CHAPTER XXII. — SUMMARY OF FACTS CONCERNING THE FIRST DAY 213-218

THE CHANGE OF THE SABBATH.

CHAPTER I.

THE SABBATH A LIVING ISSUE.

This question is agitating the public mind throughout Christendom. It is one of the leading questions of the age, and promises to become more and more important. In past centuries it has engaged public attention more or less. Theologians have often wrestled with it, and fondly thought they had settled it; but the revolving years still bring it to the surface. It will not down. Legislatures have considered it, and from time to time have placed the heavy hand of civil power in the scale to make the result decisive. Yet the public mind is not at rest; the interest in the subject revives; and it is safe to say that at the present time there is more real desire to know the whole truth upon this question than there has been at any time for a thousand years past.

The age in which we live is peculiar. There is little reverence in its spirit for the opinions of the hoary past. Everything is being investigated, and it is not surprising that the Sabbath question should have its share of public attention; the nature of the subject is such that it merits consideration. The Bible presents the Sabbath as the most ancient institution, excepting marriage, which man was to observe as a moral duty. Gen. 2:1-3. Its existence has run parallel with that of the race. Multitudes of the most intelligent and conscientious believe that its universal observance is necessary if man is to attain to his highest physical, moral, and spiritual development. The most civilized and powerful nations of the earth have even made rigorous laws to enforce a weekly rest-day upon their subjects. It comes to hundreds of millions of our race every seven days of our mortal life. It furnishes a day of worship and religious instruction to a large portion of the human family. It cannot be denied that it has furnished one of the most powerful impulses to mold our modern civilization. The importance of the subject, then, cannot be overestimated.

But the Sabbath, above all else, is a religious day. It called into being the division of time into weeks. No other cause can be found for the week, other than the appointment of a day to be observed in memory of God's work of creation. All we know of its origin we learn from Moses' record of creation in the Bible. The Gentile nations have received its benefits since their conversion from heathenism, till now it is known to earth's remotest bounds. As the Sabbath relates to God, and he appointed its rest, and made it a religious day, and all we know of its institution and moral obligation is derived from his word, the question becomes one of religious duty,—a question of conscience, relating primarily to human salvation, and but secondarily to man's physical and social welfare.

There can be no Sabbath institution unless some *day* is observed as a Sabbath. This is self-evident. Some particular day, recurring every week, must be used as a day of rest and religious observance in order to have such an institution. Since God is the author of the institution, he must, therefore, have appointed some day for its celebration. To leave any day of the seven to be observed as the Sabbath would have much the same effect as to have no Sabbath at all; the days of the week would stand upon an equality. The essence of the institution requires the appointment of a particular day of the seven as a day of rest and worship.

Did God appoint such a day? If so, what day was it? Has the original appointment continued till the present time? or has God for some important reason changed it to another day? What day is now obligatory? These are questions of great moment. In religious truth, upon which our salvation hinges, we want to know God's will. Human authority is not sufficient. In this age, everything which can be shaken will be shaken. We want to anchor to those things which will stand the test of the closest examination. It is an investigating age. Everything is being criticised. Our souls demand *the truth*. Truth will bear examination; but it is not so with error.

In the great Sabbath agitation of the present age, every point will receive the closest scrutiny by unbelievers. Christians should therefore *know* whereof they affirm. We want the divine warrant for religious institutions. Human authority is but as chaff to the wheat. What has the Lord said? should be our inquiry. "Thy word is a lamp unto my feet, and a light unto my path." "All Scripture is given by inspiration of God, . . . that the man of God may be perfect, thoroughly furnished unto all good works."

We therefore propose to investigate the subject of the Sabbath with special reference to the question, What day should we observe as the Sabbath in this age of the world? The public mind is interested in it. Thousands of children, coming to years of understanding, ask their parents why they observe the first day of the week, while the commandment requires the seventh. We want to help these parents to answer that question truly. Multitudes are perplexed upon this point; and we hope to assist somewhat in answering it. We propose to examine the Scriptures, which should ever be of primal authority; also to consider the statements of history bearing upon it, and thus give the ground a brief but faithful examination. If the Bible will thoroughly furnish us "unto all good works," it will enable us to settle this question correctly. Where shall we look for light upon it, if not to God's revealed truth? "To the law and to the testimony;" if they will not afford us light, we may look in vain to man's authority.

CHAPTER II.

THE ORIGIN OF THE SABBATH.

OUR Saviour says, "The Sabbath was made for man." Mark 2:27. The term *man* must here be used in its generic sense, comprehending the whole race. If the Sabbath, then, was made for mankind, it must have been made at the time when man himself was created; hence we must go back to the creation for the institution of the Sabbath.

The first part of Moses' record of the creation, in Gen. 1 and 2, is devoted to the origin of the weekly cycle and the Sabbath institution. Here God sets before us the result of each day's work. He carefully distinguishes between the days, stating that each was composed of an "evening and a morning,"—a dark part and a light part,—thus describing the twenty-four-hour day. After carefully enumerating the labor of six of these days, he declares that the work of creation is completed. What he did on the next day, the seventh of this first week of time, is stated in chap. 2:2, 3: "And on the seventh day God ended his work which he had made; and he rested on the seventh day from all his work which he had made. And God blessed the seventh day, and sanctified it; because that in it he had rested from all his work which God created and made." Here we have the origin of the weekly cycle, the Sabbatic institution, and the distinction between the days of the week. The Bible speaks of "the six working days" and "the Sabbath day." Eze. 46 : 1. This brief narrative in the very first record of the world's history, makes this distinction plain. God himself employed six specific days of the first week in the labor of creating, and the seventh day of that week in resting. The word "Sabbath" means *rest*.

Why did God choose to work just six days and rest the seventh? He might have made the world in a moment, or he could have employed any other amount of time in doing it. He did not rest because he was weary, for he "fainteth not, neither is weary." Isa. 40 : 28. No other reason can be assigned but this : He was laying the foundation of that glorious institution which our Saviour declares was made for the race of men, the Sabbath of the Lord.

But to bring out this point still more clearly, let us notice carefully the language we have quoted from Gen. 2 : 2, 3. The first act of God on the seventh day was to rest ; it thus became God's rest day, or Sabbath. His second act concerning it was to place his blessing upon it ; thus it became his "blessed" rest day. His third act was to "sanctify" it. *Sanctify* signifies to "set apart to a holy or religious use."—*Webster*. By this appointment, the seventh day of the week became the day of holy rest and religious observance for those for whom it was designed, until such appointment should be revoked. Notice how definite is the language : "God blessed the seventh day, and sanctified it ; because that in it he *had* rested from all his work which God created and made." The blessing and sanctification of the seventh day were not therefore bestowed upon it until that particular day on which he rested was in the past. The blessing bestowed pertained to its future recurrence as it returned in the weekly cycle. Every time it returned after this blessing was placed upon it, it was to be understood by those who reverenced God that it was his blessed day, and must not be treated as the other six days were treated. It was also "sanctified," that is, it was now the day appointed for religious uses. While it was proper to use the other six days for secular work and ordinary business, the seventh day of the week, every time it returned, was only to be used for religious purposes. All this occurred, according to the inspired record, at the close of creation week.

It is sometimes objected that we have no *command* for the observance of the seventh-day Sabbath till the giving of the law to Israel on Mount Sinai. Such objectors fail to comprehend the record in Gen. 2 : 1-3. When God sanctified the seventh day, thus appointing it to a sacred use, he must have made known this fact to Adam and Eve,—those for whose benefit it was instituted. They stood as the representatives of the race, through whom the instructions from God were to be given. We cannot conceive how God could appoint this day to this special purpose in any other way than by informing them of it.

The Hebrew verb *kadash*, here rendered *sanctified*, is defined by Gesenius, "To pronounce holy, to sanctify, . . . to institute any holy thing, to appoint." This word in the Old Testament commonly implies a public appointment by proclamation. When the cities of refuge were set apart for that particular purpose, the record states (Josh. 20:7), "They appointed (Heb. *sanctified*, margin) Kedesh in Galilee in Mount Naphtali, and Shechem in Mount Ephraim," etc. Here we see that a public announcement was made of the fact to all Israel. In Joel 1:14 another instance is furnished: "Sanctify [*i. e.* appoint] ye a fast, call a solemn assembly, gather the elders," etc. This could not be done without a public notification of the fact. When king Jehu wished to entrap the worshipers of Baal and destroy them, he made this public announcement: "Proclaim [Heb. *sanctify*, margin] a solemn assembly for Baal. And they proclaimed it." 2 Kings 10:20. It would not have been possible to make this appointment otherwise than by making the people acquainted with the fact.

But the most remarkable instance of this use of the word is found in the record of the sanctification of Mount Sinai. Ex. 19:12, 23. When the Lord was about to speak the ten commandments, he sent Moses down to command the people not to touch the mount, lest they be destroyed. "And Moses said unto the Lord, The people cannot come up to Mount Sinai; for thou chargedst us, saying, Set bounds about the mount, and *sanctify* it." Going back to verse 12, we learn how this was done. "And thou shalt set bounds unto the people round about, *saying*, Take heed to yourselves, that ye go not up into the mount, or touch the border of it." Here we see that to *sanctify* the mount was to tell the people that God would have them treat it as sacred to himself.

From these and many other instances of the use of the word *sanctify* in the Scriptures, we must understand that when God sanctified the seventh day at creation, he told Adam and Eve that it was sacred unto the Lord. The statement that "God blessed the seventh day, and sanctified it" positively proves that the Lord commanded our first parents to treat the seventh day as holy time. It is a record of that fact; for in no other way could it have been "appointed" to such a use. This fact—that God gave a commandment at the creation of the world to the representative heads of the race, to keep holy the seventh day of the week—has an important bearing upon the Sabbath question for every succeeding age.

CHAPTER III.

THE SABBATH PREVIOUS TO THE GIVING OF THE LAW.

THE giving of the law, according to Usher's chronology, was about twenty-five centuries after creation week. It is interesting to trace the Sabbath through this long, remote period. The only written history extant covering it, is the book of Genesis, with its fifty short chapters, written by Moses. The facts presented in it are invaluable. It gives us brief glimpses of the long-lived race previous to the flood, and of the rise of the most powerful nations of succeeding ages, and of the call of Abraham, with the experiences of his immediate descendants. It presents most valuable historical instruction relative to God's plan of dealing with his creatures, and the principles of his moral government. It is in no sense a book of laws, but only a very brief history of the earliest ages of antiquity.

As we have already seen, the book of Genesis commences with the origin of the weekly cycle, as brought to view in the account of creation, and the institution of the Sabbath, without which that cycle would never have existed. The division of time into days, months, and years is easily traceable to nature. The revolution of the earth on its axis, the changes of the moon, and the circuit of the earth around the sun, originate these divisions of time. But no such origin can be found for the weekly cycle. Beyond all question, it owes its existence to the act of Jehovah in setting apart the seventh day at the creation of the world. Not even a plausible conjecture has ever been found for any other origin of it. It is a well-attested historical fact that the weekly cycle existed, and the seventh day was kept sacred, by nearly all of the most ancient nations of the earth besides the Jews. There are decisive evidences which show that the Assyrians, Babylonians, Persians, Arabians, Greeks, and Romans; and even the Chinese, knew of the Sabbath, and at an early period regarded it as a sacred day. We may notice this point more fully hereafter, but will introduce brief evidences of it here.

John G. Butler, a Free-will Baptist author, in his "Natural and Revealed Theology," p. 396, says, "We learn, also, from the testimony of Philo, Hesiod, Josephus, Porphyry, and others, that the division of time into weeks, and the observance of the seventh day, were common to the nations of antiquity. They would not have adopted such a custom from the Jews. Whence, then, could it have been derived but through tradition, from its original institution in the Garden of Eden?"

The *Asiatic Journal* says:—

"The prime minister of the empire affirms that the Sabbath was anciently observed by the Chinese, in conformity to the directions of the king."

The *Congregationalist* (Boston), Nov. 15, 1882, referring to the "Creation Tablets" found by Mr. Smith on the bank of the Tigris, near Nineveh, gives the following:—

"Mr. George Smith says in his 'Assyrian Discoveries' (1875): 'In the year 1869 I discovered, among other things, a curious religious calendar of the Assyrians, in which every month is divided into four weeks, and the seventh days, or Sabbaths, are marked out as days on which no work should be undertaken. . . . The calendar contains lists of work forbidden to be done on these days, which evidently correspond to the Sabbaths of the Jews.'"

Much more testimony on this point might be presented, but this is sufficient to show that the weekly cycle and the Sabbath were extensively known among these ancient nations. Brief references to the same thing in the books of Genesis and Exodus demonstrate the existence of the week and the Sabbath previous to the giving of the law.

In the history of the deluge (Gen. 7 and 8) there are several references to the weekly division of time. Chap. 7:4: "For yet seven days, and I will cause it to rain upon the earth." Also chap. 8:10, 12: "And he stayed yet other seven days," etc. Here are three different weekly periods brought to view in this short account of the flood. It could not have been accidental that this period of seven days should be chosen three successive times. It points unmistakably to the fact that the weekly cycle was in constant use in that age of the world.

In the history of Jacob's marriage to the daughters of Laban, the week is also mentioned. Gen. 29:27, 28: "Fulfill the week of this one, and we will give thee the other also for the service which thou shalt serve with me yet seven other years. And Jacob did so, and fulfilled her week" (Revised Version). The Sabbath is inseparably connected with the weekly division of time; hence, if the week existed, the Sabbath must also have been known. We are forced to conclude, therefore, that these inhabitants of Chaldea were well acquainted with its sacred obligation. Notice the testimony, already referred to, of those tablets dug out of ancient ruins found in that country.

A decisive proof that the Sabbath was well known to the Israelites previous to the giving of the law, is found in Exodus 16:4, 5, 22-30: "Then said the Lord unto Moses, Behold, I will rain bread from heaven for you; and the people shall go out and gather a certain rate every day, that I may prove them, whether they will walk in my law, or no. And it shall come to pass, that on the sixth day they shall prepare that which they bring in; and it shall be twice as much as they gather daily." Then we have an account of the falling of the manna. He continues in verses 22–30: "And it came to pass, that on the sixth day they gathered twice as much bread, two omers for one man; and all the rulers of the congregation came and told Moses. And he said unto them, This is that which the Lord hath said, To-morrow is the rest of the holy Sabbath unto the Lord; bake that which ye will bake to-day, and seethe that ye will seethe; and that which remaineth over lay up for you to be kept until the morning. And they laid it up till the morning, as Moses bade; and it did not stink, neither was there any worm therein. And Moses said, Eat that to-day; for to-day is a Sabbath unto the Lord: to-day ye shall not find it in the field. Six days ye shall gather it; but on the seventh day, which is the Sabbath, in it there shall be none. And it came to pass, that there went out some of the people on the seventh day for to gather, and they found none. And the Lord said unto Moses, How long refuse ye to keep my commandments and my laws? See, for that the Lord hath given you the Sabbath, therefore he giveth you on the sixth day the bread of two days; abide ye every man in his place, let no man go out of his place on the seventh day. So the people rested on the seventh day."

From the foregoing language the following conclusions are inevitable:—

1. God had a law, of which the seventh-day Sabbath was a part, more than a month previous to proclaiming his commandments from Mount Sinai.

2. He proved his people by giving them bread from heaven, to see whether they would obey his law or not, that test coming on their observance of the Sabbath, which, therefore, must be a most important part of the law.

3. The language shows that the people had a knowledge of the Sabbath, and that many of them desired to keep it before any commandment whatever was given them as a people concerning it; for the record of their deliverance from Egypt does not give a single hint concerning the Sabbath, previous to this point.

4. We are constrained, therefore, to conclude that when he says, "How long refuse ye to keep my commandments and my laws?" he must refer back to the original institution of the Sabbath at creation, the knowledge of which had been preserved through the patriarchs and the general acquaintance of the ancient nations with the Sabbath.

5. The fall of the manna, which continued through the forty years of their wanderings, with its double portion on the sixth day of the week, and none upon the seventh; its being kept from corruption on the Sabbath, while it would soon spoil on other days, attested which was the true creation Sabbath at that time, and their perfect knowledge of it.

An objection is sometimes offered upon the passage, "See, for that the Lord hath given you the Sabbath," etc., that it belonged wholly to the Israelites. But surely it must have had a previous existence or it would not have been proper to say he *gave* it to them. He did this in precisely the same sense that he gave himself to that people, and thus became God of Israel. The nations had gone into idolatry, or were fast doing so, rejecting alike the true God and the great memorial of his creation work, the Sabbath. He had separated from among them the descendants of Abraham, who still regarded both. From this time on, the Sabbath and the knowledge of the true God rapidly disappeared from the nations of the earth, and they became heathen; while the Israelites remembered God and his Sabbath, and preserved the knowledge of each to be given again under more favorable auspices to the Gentile nations.

From these considerations we cannot doubt that Israel regarded the Sabbath more or less sacredly while in Egyptian bondage. Hence it is not to be supposed that the Israelites could keep it as fully while in bondage as they were able to do afterwards. But it seems unreasonable to conclude that they had lost all regard for it, or that the most pious among them gave it no respect. God says of their great progenitor, "Abraham obeyed my voice, and kept my charge, my commandments, my statutes, and my laws." We are certain that Isaac, Jacob, and Joseph followed the same example, and therefore must have kept the Sabbath. The two latter were in Egypt, and no doubt the rest of their kindred followed their example, and regarded the Sabbath as much as their circumstances would permit. They looked back to these noble patriarchs with the deepest respect. They still had a regard for the Sabbath, as we learn in Exodus 16, even before the giving of the law. Hence it was not to them a new institution.

In this brief account it has been plainly shown that the Sabbath of the Lord was given to the human family at creation, and was well known to those who had any regard for the true God. It certainly was not a Jewish institution ; for it existed, and was commanded to be observed by the God of heaven, long ages before a Jew lived. The Jews sprung from Judah, one of the sons of Jacob ; but the Sabbath was set apart in Eden for man's benefit. It was "made for man."

CHAPTER IV.

THE SABBATH AT THE GIVING OF THE LAW.

WE come now to that sublime event in the history of God's dealings with mankind, the proclamation of his law from Sinai. In the sixteenth chapter of Exodus we have the account of his giving his Sabbath to Israel; in chapter nineteen we have the full statement of his giving himself to that people by a solemn covenant; and in chapter twenty, the history of his committing his law to them. This was a wonderful honor which he conferred upon the posterity of Abraham, the friend of God. The Jews were indeed favored in this respect above all the nations of the earth. The apostle Paul inquires, "What advantage, then, hath the Jew?" and he immediately answers, "Much every way ; chiefly because that unto them were committed the oracles of God." Rom. 3 : 1, 2. But while these acts honored that people, they in no way dishonored God, or the law, or the Sabbath, nor made them Jewish.

Some thirty days after the fall of the manna commenced, all Israel were camped at the base of Sinai, waiting to hear from the mouth of Jehovah the ten commandments. The mountain burned with fire, and the smoke ascended like the smoke of a furnace. Thunderings and lightnings and the voice of a trumpet exceeding loud were seen and heard. The solid earth trembled, "and so terrible was the sight, that Moses said, I exceedingly fear and quake." The voice of God was then heard proclaiming the "ten words which, not only in the Old Testament but in all revelation, are the most emphatically regarded as the synopsis of all religion and morality."

In this law he thus speaks of the Sabbath : "Remember the Sabbath day to keep it holy. Six days shalt thou labor and do all thy work ; but the seventh day is the Sabbath of the Lord thy God ; in it thou shalt not do any work, thou, nor thy son, nor thy daughter, thy manservant, nor thy maidservant, nor thy cattle, nor thy stranger that is within thy gates. For in six days the Lord made heaven and earth, the sea, and all that in them is, and rested the seventh day ; wherefore the Lord blessed the Sabbath day, and hallowed it." Here we have a precept, "Remember the Sabbath day to keep it holy," then an explanation of the precept, and, finally, the reason why it is given. It begins with the word "Remember." The Sabbath is a commemorative institution. This word recognizes it as already existing; therefore the fourth commandment did not originate the Sabbath. It plainly points us back to the creation of the world for its beginning. "In six days the Lord made heaven and earth, the sea, and all that in them is;" "wherefore [*i. e.*, for this reason] the Lord blessed the Sabbath day, and hallowed it." The Sabbath is God's memorial of creation; hence every intelligent creature is under obligations to keep it. This is far higher than any mere Jewish reason. It existed at the birth of the race. There is nothing about the Wilderness of Sin, or the coming out of Egypt, in this original Sabbath commandment. It sets forth reasons for its observance which should convince every man and woman who lives on the earth.

How forcibly these words harmonize with the historical account in the second chapter of Genesis: "God blessed the seventh day, and sanctified it, because that in it he had rested from all his work which God created and made." In the fourth commandment he states, "For in six days the Lord made heaven and earth," etc., "and rested the seventh day; wherefore the Lord blessed the Sabbath day, and hallowed it." It would be folly and presumption to undertake to separate between the Sabbath of creation and that of the fourth commandment.

CHAPTER V.

WHAT THE FOURTH COMMANDMENT REQUIRES.

This precept simply requires that day of the week to be kept holy on which the Creator rested. This, we have learned over and over again, was the seventh day of the week. He rested on one day only of the weekly cycle, and this rest was long ages in the past when the command was given, and could not, therefore, be changed. Hence the fourth commandment can be made to sanction Sabbatizing on no other day of the week than the seventh. One cannot change his birthday. Independence day cannot be separated from the Fourth of July; for the events occurring in 1776 fix it to that point, and they cannot now be changed. So of God's rest day; the facts are such that before it could be changed, the whole work of creation would have to be gone over again. God rested on the seventh day of the first week of time. We are to rest on the same day of the week to keep that great fact in memory. What would we think of the propriety of appointing some other day besides the fourth of July to commemorate the independence of these United States? This would be no more absurd than to observe some other day than the seventh to answer the claims of the fourth commandment.

This command is inseparably connected with the day of Jehovah's rest. It is the particular day of God's rest which the command requires to be kept holy, and no other. It is not a seventh part of time that the command specifies; neither merely one day in seven after six of labor; but it is *the seventh day, on which God rested from the work of creation*, which is appointed for man to keep as it comes to him in the weekly cycle.

God was at this very time showing the people, by weekly miracles, in the fall of the manna, which day this creation Sabbath was. There could be no doubt on this point, no time lost. They then had the right day from creation. The God of all the earth was pointing it out to them every week. The true weekly cycle was therefore known at the time the law was given. Doubtless, it had always been kept by the patriarchs from the creation to this time, as it was by the Jewish people till the time of Christ.

The speaking of the law on Sinai by the Creator of the universe, and his writing it on the imperishable tablets of stone with his own finger, marks a most important epoch in the religious progress of the race. The fact that the creation Sabbath was given such great prominence as to be made the central and most extensive precept in it, demonstrates the exalted position it occupied in the Lawgiver's estimation. No satisfactory reason can be assigned for this high honor, other than that "the Sabbath," which "was made for man," was exceedingly important for his well-being. It was the day for religious benefit, for spiritual improvement,—the day in which to remember our Creator, and that we are the workmanship of his hands. Mark this fact well: the principal object of the Sabbath, according to the commandment, is not mere rest from physical toil. It is to be kept "*holy;*" for it was made holy at the creation. The facts of creation are to be remembered. Religious contemplation and rest from secular labor are the main objects of the day. It is God's day, and not ours. He has never given us this day to use for *our* purposes.

CHAPTER VI.

THE SABBATH FROM THE GIVING OF THE LAW TILL THE RESURRECTION OF CHRIST.

ALL theologians agree that during the lapse of fifteen centuries, between the giving of the law on Mount Sinai and the resurrection of our Lord, the seventh day of the week was observed with more or less strictness by the Jewish people, and was obligatory upon them by divine authority. We shall not, therefore, devote much time to its consideration during this period, but we will notice a few prominent points.

That law of which the Sabbath was a part, spoken by God upon Mount Sinai, was written by his own finger on two tables of stone, thus indicating its enduring character; and being placed within the ark in the most holy place of the sanctuary, beneath the mercy-seat, where between the cherubim, the visible presence of God rested, it was the central object of interest in their system of religion. Ex. 31:18; Deut. 4:12, 13; 5:22; 10:1-5; Ex. 40:20, 21.

The Sabbath is mentioned in various scriptures during this long period, showing that it was observed by the pious among that people; while there are many reproofs given by the sacred writers for transgressions of the Sabbath law. Neh. 10:31, 33; 2 Kings 4:23; Amos 8:4-6; Isa. 56:1-8, etc.

One striking fact showing God's regard for the Sabbath, is found in the prophecy of Jeremiah (chap. 17:20-27): "Hear ye the word of the Lord, ye kings of Judah, and all Judah, and all the inhabitants of Jerusalem, that enter in by these gates: Thus saith the Lord, Take heed to yourselves, and bear no burden on the Sabbath day, nor bring it in by the gates of Jerusalem; neither carry forth a burden out of your houses on the Sabbath day; neither do ye any work, but hallow ye the Sabbath day, as I commanded your fathers. But they obeyed not, neither inclined their ear, but made their neck stiff, that they might not hear, nor receive instruction. And it shall come to pass, if ye diligently hearken unto me, saith the Lord, to bring in no burden through the gates of this city on the Sabbath day, but hallow the Sabbath day, to do no work therein, then shall there enter into the gates of this city kings and princes sitting upon the throne of David, riding in chariots and on horses, they, and their princes, the men of Judah, and the inhabitants of Jerusalem; and this city shall REMAIN FOREVER.

And they shall come from the cities of Judah, and from the places about Jerusalem, and from the land of Benjamin, and from the plain, and from the mountains, and from the south, bringing burnt offerings, and sacrifices, and meat offerings, and incense, and bringing sacrifices of praise, unto the house of the Lord. But if ye will not hearken unto me to hallow the Sabbath day, and not to bear a burden, even entering in at the gates of Jerusalem on the Sabbath day, then will I kindle a fire in the gates thereof, and it shall devour the palaces of Jerusalem, and it shall not be quenched."

On this text Dr. Adam Clarke comments thus: "From this and the following verses we find the ruin of the Jews attributed to the breach of the Sabbath; as this led to a neglect of sacrifice, the ordinances of religion, and all public worship, so it necessarily brought with it all immorality. This breach of the Sabbath was that which let in upon them all the waters of God's wrath."

What could exalt the importance of the Sabbath more than these statements of Holy Writ? Had they kept the Sabbath sacredly, it would have brought with it other religious blessings, and would have preserved their city and nation forever; whereas their neglect of the Sabbath ultimately caused their ruin as a nation. They were very lax in its observance previous to their captivity in Babylon, and were often reproved for this. But after their return, they were much more strict; indeed, they were so particular in regard to its observance that they would sometimes suffer themselves to be overcome rather than fight on the Sabbath. They would not attack their enemies on that day, even when their neglect to do so endangered their safety. Josephus gives us many instances of this kind. ("Antiquities," b. 12, chap. 6 ; and b. 13, chap. 1 ; also the book of the Maccabees.)

Previous to the time of Christ, and after the Lord's prophets ceased to appear in their midst, the Jews became very fond of tradition, exalting it even above the authority of the Scriptures. Many instances of this kind are given in the Gospels. Christ sharply reproved the Jews on this point. There was no requirement of God more abused by tradition than the Sabbath ; indeed, it was greatly perverted from its original design by this means. Dr. Justin Edwards, in his "Sabbath Manual," pages 214, 215, gives the following list : "They enumerated about forty primary works, which they said were forbidden to be done on the Sabbath. Under each of these were numerous secondary works, which they said were also forbidden. . . . Among the primary works which were forbidden, were plowing, sowing, reaping, winnowing, cleaning, grinding, etc. Under the head of grinding was included the breaking or dividing of things which were before united. . . . Another of their traditions was, that, as threshing on the Sabbath was forbidden, the bruising of things, which was a species of threshing, was also forbidden. Of course, it was a violation of the Sabbath to walk on green grass ; for that would bruise or thresh it. So, as a man might not hunt on the Sabbath, he might not catch a flea; for that was a species of hunting. As a man might not carry a burden on the Sabbath, he might not carry water to a thirsty animal; for that was a species of burden; but he might pour water into a trough, and lead the animal to it. . . . Yet, should a sheep fall into a pit, they would readily lift him out, and bear him to a place of safety. . . . They said a man might minister to the sick for the purpose of relieving their distress, but not for the purpose of healing their diseases. He might put a covering on a diseased eye, or anoint it with eye-salve for the purpose of easing the pain, but not to cure the eye." These foolish traditions, when carried out, made the Sabbath a burdensome yoke instead of the merciful institution which God designed it should be, a delight and blessing to his creatures. How wonderfully this explains many of the references to the Sabbath in the Gospels!

The Jews found fault with Christ because he paid no respect to these traditions. But he found fault with them for making the commandments of God of none effect by their tradition. Matt. 15:4-9. The Pharisees accused him of breaking the Sabbath, because he healed the sick (Matt. 12:9-14), cast out devils (Luke 4:33-36), gave sight to the blind (John 9:1-16), permitted his disciples to pluck and rub out the wheat heads and eat (Matt. 12:1-8), and directed the man to carry his bed—a burden like a cloak or mat— (Matt. 9:1-6), on the Sabbath day.

Modern enemies to the seventh-day Sabbath have sometimes united with the ancient haters of Christ in thus accusing our Lord of being a transgressor of the law, *i. e.*, a sinner. But it will be impossible to show a single instance where he violated the Sabbath commandment. Had he done so, he would not have been sinless, he could not have been our Saviour. The law would have condemned him; for all admit that it was obligatory all through Christ's ministry till his crucifixion. We utter an emphatic protest against thus attributing disobedience to God, our only perfect Example. Just as he was about to be offered for the sins of others, he declared, "I have kept my Father's commandments." John 15:10. He certainly had not broken them if he had kept them, and the Sabbath command was one of those which he had kept.

Our Saviour constantly justified his course against the accusers, who claimed that he or his disciples had broken the Sabbath. When they complained because his disciples had plucked and eaten the wheat, he declared they were "guiltless." Matt. 12:7. "Guiltless" signifies "not guilty." They had done no wrong. They had not broken the law. They had only violated one of their human traditions. When he healed the man whose hand was withered (Matt. 12:9-14), they sought to destroy him for it; but he declares his course in thus doing well was "lawful," *i. e.*, according to law. He had done no wrong. But they had erected their traditions, as we have seen, and they were angry because he would not regard them. The time had come for him to strip off these wretched perversions of God's truth, and restore the law to its own naked purity. He says, "In vain they do worship me, teaching for doctrines the commandments of men." Matt. 15:9. Our Saviour ever exalted the law of his Father, and taught its eternal perpetuity. Matt. 5:17-20; 15:1-20; 19:16-22; 22:34-40; etc., etc. The Sabbath is an important part of this law. It was his "custom" to attend divine service on the seventh-day Sabbath, and to instruct the people. Luke 4:16. "Custom" implies a constant practice. He placed the most distinguished honor upon it, by teaching that the Sabbath was made for the race of man, and that he was its Lord. Mark 2:27, 28. It was not made merely for the Jews, but for all men. This statement recognizes its existence when man was first created. This was some twenty-three centuries before Judah, the father of the Jewish people, was born. Hence our Saviour teaches that it was in no sense a Jewish institution.

The fact that God's only begotten Son claims to be the "Lord of the Sabbath," is the highest honor which could be conferred upon it. Some in these days greatly misunderstand and pervert this important fact. They would have us believe that because he is its Lord, therefore he might conclude to set it aside, change or abolish it altogether. A strange conclusion! Christ is Lord of his people. "Ye call me Master and Lord, and ye say well, for so I am." But we do not conclude, therefore, that he will destroy or abolish his people because he is their Lord. Sarah called Abraham lord. 1 Peter 3:6. She certainly did not have the remotest idea he would destroy her because of this fact. We read of the House of Lords of England. This title of high honor does not signify that they are the destroyers of the people. The word rather implies a protector, a guardian, one who will defend the rights of those over whom he is lord.

The fact that the Son of God is Lord of the Sabbath implies that he understands its nature, origin, and rights better than any one else, and will guard them sacredly. And why should he not? Christ himself made the world. John 1:3; Col. 1:16; Heb. 1:2. He was present, and performed the very acts which laid the foundation of the Sabbath. He rested, therefore, himself from his acts of creation. He was also with the church in the wilderness when the commandments were spoken. Ex. 23:20, 21; Acts 7:37, 38; 1 Cor. 10:4. The Sabbath is, then, the Lord's day in a special sense. Thus we have traced the seventh day with an unvarying sanctity from creation to the crucifixion of Christ.

CHAPTER VII.

DID OUR SAVIOUR CHANGE THE SABBATH BEFORE HIS ASCENSION?

THERE is a general agreement among leading commentators and ministers of nearly all denominations that the Sabbath was kept in the Garden of Eden by Adam and Eve, and that it came down through the patriarchal age as an institution of Jehovah, unimpaired in its obligation, and that the commandment given on Mount Sinai simply repeats the events which occurred at the close of the first week of time. All Christians believe that the Israelites were under obligation to keep the seventh day till the resurrection of Christ; but concerning its obligation since the crucifixion, opinions widely differ. Many Christians believe that the seventh day ceased to be the Sabbath, and that the first day of the week, upon which Christ rose from the dead, took its place as the Sabbath, by divine appointment, to be kept throughout the new dispensation. Others believe that the Sabbath law was abolished, and that we have no sacred day of rest now binding upon us.

Before examining the evidence usually adduced in support of Sunday-keeping, it may be well to look briefly to the probabilities of the case. Could we reasonably expect that the Sabbath day which had been kept for four thousand years, would be set aside, and another day, hitherto used for secular purposes, substituted? This would indeed be an act requiring great changes both in the lives and in the habits of the people,—one which would attract universal attention. No one claims that the first day of the week had ever been recognized as a sacred day in any sense whatever among the Jewish people before the crucifixion of Christ. The seventh day had always, from the exode up to that point, been recognized by them as a weekly Sabbath. All admit that there never was a period in their history when it was more universally and strictly regarded than during our Saviour's ministry. Indeed, they carried their strictness to a great extreme, till it had become a burdensome yoke.

This was the condition of things at the death of Christ. And the disciples and early believers, for several years after the crucifixion, were every one of them of Jewish birth, trained from their infancy to the strictest observance of the seventh-day Sabbath. No Gentile was converted till Cornelius received a visit from St. Peter about three and a half years after the ascension. Acts 10. Now, are we to suppose that all these Jews who believed in Christ suddenly changed their Sabbath day from the one they had always observed, and yet no record whatever be made concerning it? No command whatever for them to do this is claimed by any one. We cannot conceive of anything more improbable. Within a short time after Christ's ascension, many thousands of pious Jews accepted the gospel. These not only regarded the moral law as binding, but still continued zealous observers of the ceremonial law. Many of them went so far as to teach that Gentiles must be circumcised also, and thus caused the apostles Paul and Barnabas great trouble. They were great sticklers for the rites and services of the law of Moses. Acts 15:1, 5; chap. 21:20, 21. This feeling affected some even of the apostles, so that they requested Paul himself to show his respect for these Jewish customs. They evidently considered every Jewish convert under obligation to treat the ceremonial law with deference.

Can we suppose, then, without evidence of the strongest kind, that all at once they would drop the observance of the day they had always regarded as the Sabbath, and commence to observe another which they had never kept? Consider what a great change this would imply. The Jewish people had complained bitterly of Jesus because he would not treat with respect their traditions concerning the Sabbath, and tried to make it appear that he was a Sabbath-breaker. Because he healed several persons of disease on the Sabbath day, or permitted his disciples to rub out the wheat heads when they were hungry, they made a great outcry, and tried to effect his condemnation. What shall we think, then, of the position which supposes that thousands of his disciples openly broke the Sabbath they had always kept before, and commenced the observance of the first day of the week as another Sabbath, when no complaint on the part of the Jews can be cited? And it is true that not a word of censure can be found in all the gospel history after Christ's crucifixion because of the disciples' breaking the Sabbath. When we consider that these very disciples were persecuted bitterly by the Jews, who were most glad to find any occasion against them, would not such an omission be indeed most marvelous if the apostles were not still keeping the seventh-day Sabbath? And is not this fact evidence most positive that they did continue to observe it as before?

A change in the observance of a weekly Sabbath from the one which is customary in any community, always marks as peculiar those who do so. If they rest while others are busy, it is quickly noticed; if they work while the great majority rest, they are still more conspicuous. Even in this age of lax Sunday observance, when so many pay but little regard to it, let a person commence to keep the seventh day as the Sabbath, and he will be marked for miles around. He will be watched, and his course commented upon. Ministers in their pulpits will warn their hearers of such an example. And in some instances he will be arrested, if the laws will permit of it, even while men fish and hunt openly, and railway trains run regularly, and other business is transacted.

What, then, would have been the effect at such a time of Jewish strictness in observing the seventh day, had the disciples no longer kept it, but taken up another day, never before held sacred, as the Sabbath?—Every one of them would have been arrested and brought before the magistrates, charged with Sabbath-breaking, and most likely would have been either imprisoned or stoned. The law existing and at that time universally acknowledged as in full authority, would have been on the side of the Jews. But not a single instance of the kind occurred, proving most emphatically that all these disciples continued to observe the seventh-day Sabbath as they always had, and as the people around them did. Hence it is utterly improbable that any change in the practice of Sabbath-keeping on the part of the disciples occurred at the time of Christ's resurrection.

What does the sacred record say concerning the Sabbath and first day during this time? All of the four Evangelists speak of the Sabbath and first day in close connection with Christ's resurrection. If any change of the Sabbath was ever made by divine authority, it must have been done in connection with this event. All believers in the sacredness of Sunday admit this. They claim that previous to Christ's resurrection the seventh day was the Sabbath by divine appointment; but subsequent to that event, the first day of the week was ever afterward to be observed by Christians. They teach that this change was by the authority and example of Christ himself.

The only historical record existing in our world of the events of that time, occurring in connection with our Lord's life, are the four Evangelists,—Matthew, Mark, Luke, and John. These are emphatically Christian historians. We depend on them for our knowledge of the facts concerning the life and incarnation of the Son of God. They wrote for the Christian world in all ages. They were devoted Christians themselves. They were inspired by the Holy Spirit; for Christ promised that it should bring all things to their remembrance, whatsoever he had said unto them. John 14:26. These things they wrote for our instruction; and we must suppose they call things by their right names, and use language correctly, else their writings would not be reliable. It is supposed by the best authorities that Matthew wrote his Gospel about six years after Christ's ascension; Mark, about ten years; Luke, about twenty-eight years; and John, about sixty-three years after that event. These historians, then, were Christians, writing for the Christians of all ages, and writing, too, many years after the Christian dispensation had begun, giving all the facts essential to a perfect understanding of the doctrines of the gospel. Do they give us to understand that any change of the Sabbath had occurred, and that the first day of the week had now become the weekly Sabbath by Christ's appointment, while the seventh day had ceased to be such? Had such a change occurred, they were surely aware of it; and if they do not mention it, we may be sure no such change had been made. We will now notice every instance in which they speak of these two days in connection with Christ's resurrection.

Matt. 28:1: "In the end of the Sabbath, as it began to dawn toward the first day of the week, came Mary Magdalene and the other Mary to see the sepulcher." Sunday-keepers claim that six years before this was written, the Sabbath was changed and the first day of the week made the Sabbath. But Matthew states that the day *before* the first day was the Sabbath, and that the first day of the week did not come till the *end* of the Sabbath. Did the Spirit of God, speaking through this Christian historian, tell the truth? If so, the day before the first day of the week, viz., the seventh day, was still the Sabbath. Surely, nothing is said by this Evangelist implying any change.

Mark gives this statement: "And when the Sabbath was past, Mary Magdalene, and Mary the mother of James, and Salome, had bought sweet spices, that they might come and anoint him. And very early in the morning, the first day of the week, they came unto the sepulcher at the rising of the sun." "Now when Jesus was risen early the first day of the week, he appeared first to Mary Magdalene, out of whom he had cast seven devils." Chap. 16 : 1, 2, 9. These words, written some ten years after the events recorded, state that the Sabbath was *past* before the first day of the week commenced. First-day writers tell us that Mark, with the other disciples, had been keeping the first day of the week as the Sabbath for ten years when he wrote this language. Can we believe such a statement? Would he apply "Sabbath" to a day which he did not regard as such, and refrain from calling the one "Sabbath" which he *did* observe? This would be most surprising, yea, utterly unreasonable. We must conclude that Mark still acknowledged the ancient Sabbath as identical with the one he observed.

Luke speaks of these days as follow: "And that day was the preparation, and the Sabbath drew on. And the women also, which came with him from Galilee, followed after, and beheld the sepulcher, and how his body was laid. And they returned, and prepared spices and ointments; and rested the Sabbath day according to the commandment. Now upon the first day of the week, very early in the morning, they came unto the sepulcher, bringing the spices which they had prepared, and certain others with them." Luke 23:54-56; 24:1.

Over twenty years after the supposed change of the Sabbath, this historian, perfectly conversant with the facts of gospel history (Luke 1:3), makes these statements: 1. The day previous to the first day of the week was the Sabbath; 2. It was the "Sabbath day according to the commandment;" 3. The holy women, the affectionate companions of Christ, still kept it as such; 4. They did things on the first day of the week they would not do on the Sabbath; *i. e.*, came to do the laborious work of embalming a dead body, thus showing conclusively that they had learned as yet of no sacredness being attached to Sunday.

From these plain facts we must conclude, first, that Luke had not been keeping Sunday as the Sabbath during the twenty years since Christ's crucifixion, or he would have given it that title, and not called the day before it such. Secondly, If the day before the first day of the week was the "Sabbath day according to the commandment," as Inspiration says, then most certainly the commandment does not at the same time require or authorize us to keep Sunday. The same command does not require us to keep two different days. "Remember the Sabbath day to keep it holy;" "The seventh day is the Sabbath of the Lord thy God," consequently Sunday is *not* the Sabbath according to the commandment. Thirdly, This commandment does have an authoritative existence this side of the cross of Christ; for it still required these women to rest on the seventh day. It had not expired when Christ was crucified, nor had it been "nailed to the cross;" for an abolished commandment can require nothing. If it existed one day this side of the cross, it still exists; and no one claims it was abolished unless done at the cross. Therefore, the law requiring the observance of the seventh-day Sabbath still exists. Nothing whatever in this connection indicates any change of the Sabbath.

John speaks as follows: "The first day of the week cometh Mary Magdalene early, when it was yet dark, unto the sepulcher, and seeth the stone taken away from the sepulcher." "Then the same day at evening, being the first day of the week, when the doors were shut where the disciples were assembled for fear of the Jews, came Jesus and stood in the midst, and saith unto them, Peace be unto you." John 20:1, 19. These words were written by the "beloved disciple" over sixty years after the resurrection of our Lord, after nearly all the other disciples who were personally acquainted with our Saviour had passed away. If he had been keeping Sunday as the only true Sabbath, or giving it any divine honor during this time, who can believe he would not have indicated it in some way? But he does not; he simply calls it by its usual secular title,—the one by which it had been known for four thousand years. He attaches no sacredness to it whatever. He does not call it the Sabbath or the Lord's day, and gives no command for its observance, not a hint of any superiority above the working days; nor do any of these writers.

There are certain claims put forth by first-day writers concerning this last-mentioned instance, which we will notice in due time. We know of no first-day advocate who claims to find any evidence of Sunday sacredness, or of a change of the Sabbath, in any of these six instances where the first day of the week is mentioned, except the one last quoted. If the Sabbath was changed, is this not surprising? If it was ever changed by divine authority, here is the point where all admit the change must have been wrought; yet none of the Christian historians who give any record of the events where this change is supposed to have occurred, ever mention such a change, or give a single hint of it. They wrote at different periods for about two thirds of a century, and gave an account of all the events in Christ's life and all his teachings which the Holy Spirit thought necessary for the proper instruction of the generations to come, but failed entirely to mention or notice any change of the Sabbath. On the contrary, they state positively, over and over, that that day was still the Sabbath which had been since God instituted it.

We may well inquire at this point, Why should any person suppose the Son of God would desire to change the creation Sabbath? This day was a memorial of the Creator, given to man as soon as he was made, to be kept, and was perpetuated through all the patriarchal ages. Placed in God's moral law of ten commandments by the Creator himself, proclaimed by his voice and written by his finger in the imperishable tablets of stone, deposited in the ark under the mercy-seat—the very center of that whole system of worship—in the most holy place of the sanctuary and temple, honored as God's day for four thousand years,—why should Christ desire to change it for another day? Was there lack of sympathy and union between the Father and the Son? Jesus says, "I and my Father are one." John 10:30. He prayed that his disciples might be one as he and his Father are. John 17:11, 21. This oneness is not in personality, but in purpose, in union. They are perfectly united in all they do. Would the Son then set aside his Father's memorial, and institute another to take its place?

The prophet declares that the Messiah "will magnify the law, and make it honorable." Isa. 42:21. The Sabbath was an important part of that law. Would he make the law honorable in abolishing the Sabbath, which was a part of it, or changing it to another day? Such changes would disgrace rather than honor it. It would be a strange way to make a thing honorable, by putting it out of existence.

When the Messiah came, he declared that he did not come to destroy the law. "Till heaven and earth pass, one jot or one tittle shall in no wise pass from the law, till all be fulfilled. Whosoever, therefore, shall break one of these least commandments, and shall teach men so, he shall be called the least [or be of no esteem, as Whiting translates it] in the kingdom of heaven." Matt. 5:17–

19. Therefore every portion of the law, of which the Sabbath is a part, shall continue till the heavens pass away. This must include the Sabbath which that law enjoins. Thus our Saviour magnified the law, every part of it.

He declares he "kept his Father's commandments." John 15 : 10. Is not his example to be followed by all his disciples? He declares himself "the Lord of the Sabbath," and says it was "made for man." Mark 2 : 27, 28. The word "Lord" here must be used in the sense of protector or guardian, and not destroyer. Sarah called Abraham "lord" (1 Peter 3 : 6); she certainly did not mean that he was her destroyer. We call Christ "our Lord;" we mean he has authority over us, cares for us, and looks after our welfare. This was what he intended to do for the Sabbath, according to this statement. Most assuredly, then, he did not abolish it, or set it aside, or change it for a secular day.

But would not Christ desire to change the Sabbath to the first day of the week, that he might have a memorial set apart to commemorate his own work? Many claim this. We reply, The seventh-day Sabbath answered this very purpose. Who was the active agent in making this world, in calling into existence this creation?—The Son of God. He it was who "made the worlds." Heb. 1 : 2. "For by him were all things created, that are in heaven, and that are in earth." Col. 1 : 16. God "created all things by Jesus Christ." Eph. 3 : 9. "All things were made" by Christ, the Word. John 1 : 3. Therefore the seventh-day Sabbath, which is a memorial of the work of creation, Christ himself taking six days in which to perform this grand origination, commemorates the work of the Son as much as that of the Father. We thus see beauty and propriety in the language of Jesus, when calling himself the "Lord of the Sabbath." The miserable perversion of the institution by the Jewish traditions, from an institution of gratitude, mercy, and refreshment, to a burdensome yoke, demanded such action from one of the founders of the Sabbath.

One of the last instructions of our Lord to his disciples, about two days before his crucifixion, shows his interest in them and his solicitude for the Sabbath: "Pray ye that your flight be not in the winter, neither on the Sabbath day." Matt. 24:20. He was foretelling the terrible destruction of Jerusalem, and giving his disciples directions how to escape it. Eleven hundred thousand Jews, rejecting that instruction, miserably perished. He says, "When ye shall see Jerusalem compassed with armies, then know that the desolation thereof is nigh." Luke 21:20. Some little time previous to the final surrounding of Jerusalem by the Roman army under Vespasian and Titus, this sign was fulfilled. Cestius, another general, did compass Jerusalem with a Roman army, and according to Josephus ("Jewish Wars," book 2, chap. 19) might easily have taken it; but "he retired from the city without any reason." Whereupon, every Christian left the city, and fled away to Pella, sixty miles distant. When the

Romans returned to invest the city, the disciples were in safety.

Christ foretold this event, and instructed them to pray that the time of this flight might not occur upon the Sabbath day or during the winter season. In the latter case it would have involved much suffering, as they were to go in the greatest haste. No other reason can be given why they were instructed to pray that their flight might not be on the Sabbath, than the Lord's desire that they should not be compelled to break it in order to escape. For nearly forty years, the disciples in Judea, as instructed by the Lord of the Sabbath, were to plead with God that their flight might not occur on the Sabbath. This proves, 1. That there was to be a Sabbath in the year A. D. 70, when Jerusalem was destroyed; 2. That this was certainly the Sabbath which was in existence when Christ spoke these words, viz., the seventh-day Sabbath, as it would be most absurd to suppose that Christ spoke of any other day than the one they were then keeping; 3. That we have here the strongest indication of the Saviour's desire that his disciples should keep the ancient Sabbath after the Christian dispensation had commenced. If he wished *them* to keep it, is not his desire just as great that *we* should keep it? Could such an injunction be found in the words of Christ, that the disciples should thus regard Sunday, how eagerly would first-day observers claim it as evidence in their favor!

In view of these considerations, we again ask, Why should any one conclude that Christ had the remotest idea of instituting another Sabbath, and setting aside the ancient Sabbath of four thousand years' standing? No intimation of it is given in a word of his or of his historians. That ancient Sabbath had answered all the wants of God's patriarchs, prophets, and holy men for all these ages. He had told the Jews that if they would keep it sacred, their city should stand forever. Jer. 17:25. Christ himself had observed it all his life, as had all his disciples. What reason can be assigned for its being changed? Do not Christians as well as Jews need to keep in mind the great work of creation? We must conclude, therefore, that no such change occurred.

CHAPTER VIII.

CONSIDERATION OF REASONS ASSIGNED FOR SUNDAY SACREDNESS.

WE will now briefly notice the leading reasons given for the supposed change of the Sabbath. We quote John 20:19: "Then the same day at evening, being the first day of the week, when the doors were shut where the disciples were assembled for fear of the Jews, came Jesus and stood in the midst, and saith unto them, Peace be unto you." It is supposed by many that these disciples were assembled to commemorate the resurrection of Jesus, and that when he came among them and said, "Peace be unto you," he indicated his approval of their act in assembling upon that day, and thus honored the first "Christian Sabbath." But does the language justify such an inference? From this and other scriptures we draw these conclusions:—

1. The reason the disciples were together was "for fear of the Jews," and not to celebrate Christ's resurrection. 2. The place of their meeting was undoubtedly the upper room, where they all abode (Acts 1:13), and not the temple or any other house of worship. 3. The time of this meeting must have been very late in the day, just before sunset. (By the Bible mode of reckoning time, the day closed at evening, or sundown. Gen. 1:5; Lev. 23:32; Mark 1:32.) We are forced to this conclusion from the facts stated by the other Evangelists, and because St. John declares it was evening. Luke gives an account of the journey of two disciples to Emmaus, seven and a half miles, that very afternoon, and of how Jesus made himself known to them "as they sat at meat," after conversing with them and explaining the Scripture predictions concerning himself. Then "he vanished out of their sight." This was "toward evening," and "the day was far spent." Then they "returned to Jerusalem, and found the eleven gathered together, and them that were with them." As they spoke of what had transpired, Jesus appeared. This must be the identical meeting spoken of by John, for he uses the same expression, "Peace be unto you," and it was at the same time of day. He then asked them, "Have ye here any meat?" and ate in their presence. Mark records the same meeting. He gives a brief

account of the two as they walked and went into the country, and of his appearing unto them; and states that the other disciples did not believe them. "Afterward he appeared unto the eleven as they sat at meat, and upbraided them with their unbelief and hardness of heart, because they believed not them which had seen him after he was risen." Mark 16:12-14. 4. We are forced to conclude that they could not have been celebrating or honoring Christ's resurrection, for they did not believe it had occurred. 5. We can see clearly how the disciples regarded this first day of the week, as two of them walked to Emmaus and back, a distance of fifteen miles, and Jesus made the same journey, and not a hint did he give that such a use of the day was wrong. A strange way to celebrate the day, if it was the first "Christian Sabbath"! They simply regarded it as a secular day, and nothing more.

The little flock of disciples were in a retired place, fearing the Jews, who had just crucified their Lord. A few of their number ventured out to the sepulcher to embalm the Saviour's body, and were astonished to find that it was not there. A few others went into the country. What a contrast to the origin of the Sabbath of the Lord! The Creator "rested" upon it himself; then he "blessed" it, and set it apart to a sacred use, evidently by telling Adam how to keep it. His example and command were both given in its favor. But how different with this first day, on which Christ rose! If there is any divine authority for keeping Sunday, this day must have been the first of the new order of Sabbaths. But it was a busy day. Christ gave no example of resting upon it; he gave no command for his disciples to rest, nor did he hold any religious service on that day. Some of his disciples traveled fifteen miles on foot upon it, he keeping them company in thus laboring. Not a hint is given in all the Bible that it should be used in any other manner than as a day for labor. Who can believe that God would in such a manner set aside the ancient Sabbath of his own appointment, and put in its place a new day, never giving a hint that the old one was abolished or the new inaugurated?

We next notice the claim that it was *customary* for Christ to meet with his disciples on the first day of the week, thus giving evidence of his regard for it, and proof of its sacredness. "And after eight days again his disciples were within, and Thomas with them; then came Jesus, the doors being shut, and stood in the midst, and said, Peace be unto you." John 20:26.

This scripture, in connection with the one just noticed, is relied upon to prove that it was the practice of Jesus to meet with his disciples on the first day of the week, between his resurrection and his ascension. It will be noticed that the record does not say that it was on the first day of the week when Christ had this interview with Thomas and the disciples. The statement is that it was "after eight days" from the previous meeting. That previous meeting was at the *very close* of the first day, most of it probably occurring on the day following. It is claimed that the expression "after eight days" signifies just a week. But what proof is there of this? "After seven days" is the expression employed by Inspiration when defining a week. Compare 1 Chron. 9:25 with 2 Kings 11:5. The expression "after six days" (Matt. 17:1) is given by another writer, "about an eight days after." Luke 9:28. On what grounds, then, shall we conclude that "after eight days" really means seven days or less? From the closing hour of Sunday, a period of time covered by the expression "after eight days," if the language be taken literally, would reach at least to the Monday night or Tuesday morning of the next week. How, then, can one rightfully claim that this meeting occurred on the first day of the week? It must be evident that this meeting was held because of the presence of Thomas, who was absent on the previous occasion, and not to honor any particular day of the week. Had the latter object been in view, the record would most certainly tell us what day of the week it was, and not use such an indefinite expression as "after eight days."

But even if we grant all our first-day friends claim, viz., that the meeting in question did occur on the first day of the week, what evidence is thereby furnished in behalf of Sunday sacredness? Our Saviour ascended to heaven on Thursday, just forty days from his resurrection. Acts 1:3. Another prominent meeting held with his disciples was on a fishing occasion. John 21:3-25. This was the third occasion that Christ manifested himself to his disciples. Verse 14. Our friends will hardly claim that this visit occurred on Sunday.

There were five first-days between the crucifixion and the ascension. No mention whatever is made of any of these five first-days, excepting the first one, on which he rose from the dead. If we admit that "after eight days" occurred on the second of those five first-days, which we are sure is not true, what could that prove? The evidence would then come far short of proving a custom, since the two following meetings—the fishing occasion and the ascension—were not on that day. A "custom" is a long-continued practice. More than two instances are required to constitute a "custom." The "custom" of our Saviour was to honor the Sabbath of the Lord, and teach the people on that day. Luke 4:16. It is utterly impossible to establish such a custom of his with reference to Sunday.

The pouring out of the Holy Spirit on the day of pentecost is supposed by many to be an evidence in favor of first-day sacredness. The Bible record is as follows: "And when the day of pentecost was fully come, they were all with one accord in one place. And suddenly there came a sound from heaven as of a rushing mighty wind, and it filled all the house where they were sitting." Acts 2:1, 2.

It is well to notice that not a word is said in the text about the first day of the week. Yet this is regarded by the adherents of Sunday sacredness as one of the strongest evidences in its behalf. It is claimed that the disciples were assembled on this first-day Sabbath, and that the Lord poured out his Spirit in honor of the day and of their act, thus adding to its sanctity. To this claim we answer: 1. There is no evidence whatever that there was any first-day Sabbath at that time to commemorate. 2. Their being assembled on that day was nothing more than had occurred on each of the previous nine days, as they were all commanded by the Saviour, "Tarry ye in the city of Jerusalem, until ye be endued with power from on high." Luke 24:49. They had been thus waiting "with one accord in prayer and supplication," about one hundred and twenty in number. Acts 1:12-26. 3. There is no hint from the connection that this occurred on the first day of the week. If the object of God had been to honor that day, he most assuredly would have given us information that the occurrence transpired then. 4. This outpouring of the Holy Spirit came, evidently, as the antitype of the feast of pentecost. This is doubtless the reason why that day is mentioned.

A strong effort is made by some to prove that pentecost came that year upon the first day of the week, though this is disputed by a large number of the ablest authors, themselves observers of Sunday. The word pentecost signifies "the fiftieth," so many days being reckoned from the passover. Olshausen, the celebrated German commentator, says: "Now since, according to the accounts given regarding the time of the feast, the passover, in the year of our Lord's death, fell so that the first day of the feast lasted from Thursday evening at six o'clock till Friday evening at the same hour, it follows, of course, that it was from Friday evening at six o'clock that the fifty days began to be counted. The fiftieth day fell, therefore, it appears, upon Saturday." Jennings, in "Jewish Antiquities," concludes his arguments by saying, "The day of pentecost must fall on the Saturday, or the Jewish Sabbath." Dr. Albert Barnes says: "If the views of the Pharisees were followed, and the Lord Jesus had with them kept the passover on Thursday, as many have supposed, then the day of pentecost would have occurred on the Jewish Sabbath, that is, on Saturday. It is impossible to determine the truth on this subject." Dean Alford in his "New Testament for English Readers," says: "The question on what day of the week this day of pentecost was, is beset with the difficulties attending the question of our Lord's last passover. . . . It appears probable, however, that it was on the Sabbath, *i. e.*, if we reckon from Saturday, the 16th of Nisan." Prof. H. B. Hackett, D. D., professor of Biblical Literature in Newton Theological Institute, in his "Commentary on the Original Text of the Acts," p. 40, thus remarks: "It is generally supposed that this pentecost, signalized by the outpouring of the Spirit, fell on the Jewish Sabbath, our Saturday." Other eminent authors — Lightfoot, Kuinöl, Hitzig, Wiesler, etc. — take the same position. We conclude, therefore, that taking the authority of first-day authors themselves, it cannot be established that pentecost came upon the first day of the week at this time, and if it could be so established, it would be no evidence in behalf of Sunday sacredness.

Another claim made in behalf of the first-day Sabbath is this: Redemption is greater than creation, therefore we should observe the day of Christ's resurrection in preference to that of the Creator's rest. In reply we would say, that this is merely human opinion. Not a syllable of Scripture can be found to sustain it. Who knows that redemption is greater than creation, since both require omnipotent power? Is man prepared to decide the comparative greatness of works that he is wholly powerless to perform, and of which he cannot have any adequate conception? And who knows that God would have us keep a Sabbath to celebrate redemption? Not a hint has he given us in his word to that effect. Would he not have told us so, had he wished us to do it? Paul says that the Holy Scriptures thoroughly furnish us unto all good works. 2 Tim. 3:17. As the keeping of Sunday as a Sabbath in honor of the work of redemption is in no instance implied in God's word, we must conclude that it is not a "good work." Every religious institution of divine appointment, has for it the authority of God's word. But there is none for the observance of a day to commemorate redemption. Such observance must therefore be merely "*will worship.*" But we inquire, Is redemption yet completed?—Certainly not, while our earth groans under the curse, and the people of God are either waiting in the grave for the final resurrection, or are living in a world of wickedness, longing for immortality. It is most surely out of place to appoint a memorial to commemorate a work yet unfinished. Christ our Advocate still intercedes for us, while we "groan within ourselves, waiting for the adoption, to wit, the redemption of our body." Rom. 8:23. Our friends are at least eighteen centuries too early in appointing their redemption Sabbath.

And even if a day were to be appointed to commemorate Christ's work in redemption at his first advent, should it not be the day of his crucifixion rather than of his resurrection? The Bible nowhere says we have redemption through his resurrection; but it does say, "In whom we have redemption through his *blood*." Eph. 1:7. Again, "Thou wast slain, and hast redeemed us to God by thy blood." Rev. 5:9. Christ shed his blood (the great agent in our redemption) on Friday, the sixth day of the week. The death of Christ is the most marvelous event ever beheld in this world. It is not surprising that God should raise his Son from the grave after he had died for the sins of men; but it is mercy most astonishing that he should ever consent that his "only begotten Son" should die that ignominious death on the cross. Shall we therefore keep Friday as a Sabbath to commemorate this sublime act of mercy and love?—Oh, no! God has instituted his own memorials to commemorate this as well as other important events. The Lord's supper answers this purpose. "For as often as ye eat this bread, and drink this cup, ye do show the Lord's death till he come." 1 Cor. 11 : 26. In baptism we have a beautiful and appropriate memorial of Christ's burial and resurrection. "Know ye not, that so many of us as were baptized into Jesus Christ, were baptized into his death? Therefore we are buried with him by baptism into death ; that *like as Christ was raised up from the dead* by the glory of the Father, even so we also should walk in newness of life. For if we have been planted together in the likeness of his death, we shall be also in the likeness of his resurrection." Rom. 6 : 3–5 ; Col. 2 : 12. How beautifully fitting is this act to commemorate Christ's resurrection!

We shall find, if we investigate the subject of God's memorials in his word, that there is always peculiar fitness—a likeness, a similarity—between the memorial and the thing commemorated by it. This principle is illustrated by the creation Sabbath, the rest signifying a completed work ; the rite of circumcision, a circle cut in the flesh, may signify the surrounding of Abraham's seed with peculiar providences as his peculiar people ; the feast of the passover and the sprinkling of the blood, bringing forcibly to view the fleeing out of Egypt, and the act of the destroying angel in passing over the houses of the children of Israel, thus saving their first-born ; the feast of tabernacles, bringing to view their dwelling in tents ; the joyful sending of gifts in the feast of purim, the gladness felt at their escape from the malice of Haman. So of the Lord's supper and baptism. Every Bible memorial is appropriate.

But how about this man-made memorial of Sunday-keeping? What fitness is there in keeping as a Sabbath a day of rest every seven days to celebrate the resurrection of Christ, as a part of the work of redemption, yet incomplete? We have seen that the resurrection day was a busy one. The disciples hunted here and there to find Christ, two of them traveling fifteen miles on foot, Jesus doing the same. It was a day of anxiety, for they did not believe he was risen until just as the day was closing. So there could have been no religious meetings or public speaking. What likeness is there between the day most Christians keep as a Sabbath, and the original day they propose to keep in memory by it? In order for it to be a fitting memorial, it should be true that the work of redemption occupied six days, and that Christ rested the day following—something no person ever claimed. As baptism is a memorial of Christ's resurrection, we would in that case have two memorials of the same event—a thing unprecedented in the Scriptures. We therefore conclude that the claim that Sunday is set apart to commemorate redemption, is absurd, and entirely contrary to the facts in the case.

CHAPTER IX.

THE SABBATH DURING THE LIVES OF THE APOSTLES.

THE Acts of the Apostles is supposed to have been written over thirty years after the resurrection of Christ. The book contains the principal historical facts of the apostolic church in the days when Christians had the greatest purity and most glorious success. It has been an invaluable treatise to all Christians for eighteen centuries. In it is given a practical illustration of the principles of gospel religion, exemplified in the labors of all the apostles, and it is in this book that we obtain a view of their understanding of Christ's teaching; for they continued to teach and enforce what they had learned from him. They did not claim to originate new doctrines. They were to go "into all the world, and preach the gospel" that they had learned from Christ.

What was their attitude toward the Sabbath? Did they treat it as an existing institution, as sacred writers in the Old Testament treated it, and as Christ and themselves had done previous to the resurrection? Or did they call the first day of the week the Sabbath, and enforce that as a new institution, taking the place of the ancient Sabbath? Most certainly if Sunday did thus enter into the place of the creation Sabbath at the resurrection of Christ, the historical record of the first thirty years would give many instances where this new Sabbath is mentioned, and it would narrate conflicts between the adherents of the new day and the old, and tell of the struggles this new day had to obtain a position as a Sabbath. We should have statements of efforts of leading men in the church, instructing the people concerning the importance of their keeping sacredly the new day, and have many references to it. We should have some command given concerning it, and plain statements of its binding obligation. Such was the case with other ordinances, doctrines, and requirements which came into force with the gospel dispensation. For example, notice baptism. Christ commands it. Matt. 28:19; Mark 16:16. St. Peter does the same. Acts 2:38; 10:48. Many instances of its performance are given in which the mode, administration, and necessity of it are intimated. Acts 8:12, 36–38; 16:33; 22:16; Rom. 6:3–5; Col. 2:12, etc. The Lord's supper was instituted by Christ himself, and commanded by divine authority. Matt. 26:26–29; Mark 14:22–25; Luke 22:15–17; 1 Cor. 11:20–26. Other illustrations of the same principle might be presented.

Do we find such illustrations of the obligation of Sunday-keeping? All its adherents claim that it originated with the Christian dispensation. Not a single command can be found for it, not an instance where it was observed as a Sabbath, not a hint that Christ had bestowed upon it any sanctity. Indeed, it is mentioned only once in the whole book of Acts: "And we sailed away from Philippi after the days of unleavened bread, and came unto them to Troas in five days; where we abode seven days. And upon the first day of the week, when the disciples came together to break bread, Paul preached unto them, ready to depart on the morrow, and continued his speech until midnight. And there were many lights in the upper chamber, where they were gathered together. And there sat in a window a certain young man named Eutychus, being fallen into a deep sleep; and as Paul was long preaching, he sunk down with sleep, and fell down from the third loft, and was taken up dead. And Paul went down, and fell on him, and embracing him said, Trouble not yourselves; for his life is in him. When he therefore was come up again, and had broken bread, and eaten, and talked a long while, even till break of day, so he departed. And they brought the young man alive, and were not a little comforted. And we went before to ship, and sailed unto Assos, there intending to take in Paul; for so had he appointed, minding himself to go afoot. And when he met with us at Assos, we took him in, and came to Mitylene." Chap. 20:6-14. We give this narrative in full, because it is considered by first-day observers as one of the strongest evidences in behalf of Sunday. This is the only instance given in the New Testament where a religious meeting is said to have been held on the first day of the week.

We learn from this scripture and its connection the following facts: This was a night meeting, "many lights" being necessary, as it continued till daybreak; Eutychus fell out of the window about midnight, Paul went down and healed him, after which he continued to speak till daylight, then departed on his journey to Assos, nineteen and a half miles distant, crossing the peninsula; Luke and his companions, with the ship, "went before," *i. e.*, started earlier, intending to go around this point of land, and take in Paul when he reached Assos. In this way Paul gained several hours in which he could speak to the disciples. To correctly understand this narrative, it becomes important to ascertain whether this meeting occurred on what we now call Saturday night or on Sunday night. It is very easily shown that it must have been the former. We have already stated that in the Bible reckoning of time the civil day commenced at the going down of the sun. "The evening and the morning were the first day" (Gen. 1:5), and the same statement is made of other days of the creation week also. The Bible is consistent with itself throughout on this subject, and it is impossible to find in it any other time for beginning the civil day. "From even unto even shall ye celebrate your Sabbath." Lev. 23:32. The Sabbath commenced at the same time as the other days. The evening began at the going down of the sun. "At even, when the sun did set." Mark 1:32.

No intelligent person will dispute the fact that the Jews, from time immemorial to the present day, have begun the civil day at the going down of the sun. The "Bible Dictionary" of the American Tract Society says, "The Hebrews began their day in the evening." We use Roman time, which came into vogue among Christians some centuries this side of the Christian era. What, then, must we conclude?—In order for this night meeting to have been on the first day of the week, it would be on what we call Saturday night. That first day began at sundown. These facts, then, must follow: Paul traveled on foot to Assos, nineteen and one half miles, during the daytime of that Sunday; and Luke and his companions spent still more of the hours of that day in traveling to the same place by ship. This conclusion is inevitable from the record. It is so plain that a large number of first-day observers have felt compelled to admit its truthfulness. Certainly they would not have done so if they had not been convinced of it. We quote from a few of them as follows:—

H. B. Hackett, D. D., Professor of Biblical Literature in Newton Theological Institution, in his comments on Acts 20:7, says: "The Jews reckoned the day [in its broad sense. Gen. 1:5] from evening to evening, and on that principle the evening of the first day of the week would be our Saturday evening. If Luke reckons so here, as many commentators suppose, the apostle then waited for the expiration of the Jewish Sabbath, and held his last religious service with the brethren at Troas at the beginning of the Christian Sabbath, *i. e.*, on Saturday evening, and consequently resumed his journey on Sunday morning." Prof. Hackett tries, however, to make it appear that Luke reckons according to the pagan method in this instance.

Dr. John Kitto says: "The evening of the first day of the week would be our Saturday evening. If Luke reckoned so here, as many commentators suppose, the apostle then waited for the expiration of the Jewish Sabbath, and held his last religious service with the brethren at Troas at the beginning of the Christian Sabbath, *i. e.*, on Saturday evening, and consequently resumed his journey on Sunday morning."—*Cyclopedia of Biblical Literature*, art. Lord's Day.

In Conybeare and Howson's "Life and Epistles of the Apostle Paul," it is said, speaking of this meeting, "It was the evening which succeeded the Jewish Sabbath. On the Sunday morning the vessel was about to sail." And of the journey that day it says: "He [Paul] pursued his lonely road that Sunday afternoon in spring, among the oak woods and the streams of Ida."—People's edition of 1878, p. 629. Prof. McGarvey, of the Disciple (Church of Christ) denomination, says: "I conclude, therefore, that the brethren met on the night after the Jewish Sabbath, which was still observed as a day of rest by all of them who were Jews or Jewish proselytes; and considering this the beginning of the first day of the week, spent it in the manner above described. On Sunday morning Paul and his companions resumed their journey."—*Commentary on Acts*.

Other authors might be quoted; but let it be noticed that these are all writers who observe Sunday themselves. They would not make these admissions unless their sense of truth required it. They express the fact that "many commentators" hold the same opinion. Prof. McGarvey admits that all the Jewish disciples and proselytes still regarded the Sabbath sacredly as a day of rest. That was in the year 59, some twenty-six years after the resurrection. According to the Bible chronology, all the apostles, Paul included, with all the companions of Christ, still regarded the seventh day as sacred. Surely this is a good admission, coming from a first-day commentator. These apostles had not learned, then, that another Sabbath had taken its place.

We see, therefore, that this scripture, which on the whole is regarded as the strongest text to be found in the Bible in behalf of Sunday, proves just the opposite from what it is cited to prove. This instance is really the second mention of the first day of the week we have seen thus far in the historical record, the day of Christ's resurrection being the first. Then some of the disciples walked fifteen miles. Here the great apostle to the Gentiles travels on foot nineteen and one half miles, while his companions travel still farther on the ship. It is strange that such instances should be thought to furnish evidence in behalf of the institution of a new Sabbath.

Should any desire to imitate apostolic example concerning Sunday, they should hold meetings on Saturday night, and work during the light part of the day ; for this is precisely what Paul and his companions did.

We have now noticed every instance where the first day of the week is mentioned in the New Testament, excepting one, which we here present: "Now concerning the collection for the saints, as I have given order to the churches of Galatia, even so do ye. Upon the first day of the week let every one of you lay by him in store, as God hath prospered him, that there be no gatherings when I come." 1 Cor. 16 : 1, 2.

This scripture is claimed as evidence for Sunday, on the ground that public collections were taken up on that day; hence there must have been public meetings held. Therefore the first day of the week was the day for public assemblies of Christians. But does this language say that public collections were taken up on the first day of the week? The whole question turns upon the expression, "lay by him in store." Would the act of taking money from the purse or pocket and placing it in a box or plate, be laying by him, *i. e.*, by himself?—Most certainly it would be just the opposite; it would be putting the money away from himself. The money would be gone. This is evidently an act to be done, not in a public gathering, but at home. This is most certainly the meaning of the original Greek. Various translations collected by J. W. Morton, late Presbyterian missionary to Hayti, read as follows: "Greenfield, in his Lexicon, translates the Greek term, 'by one's self, *i. e.*, at home;' two Latin versions, the Vulgate and that of Castellio, render it 'with one's self, at home;' three French translations, those of Martin, Osterwald, and De Sacy, 'at his own house, at home;' the German of Luther, 'by himself, at home;' the Dutch the same as the German; the

Italian of Diodati, 'in his own presence, at home;' the Spanish of Felipe Scio, 'in his own house;' the Portuguese of Ferreira, 'with himself;' the Swedish, 'near himself.' Dr. Bloomfield renders it 'by him, Fr., *chez soi*, at home;' the Douay Bible, "Let every one of you put apart with himself." Mr. Sawyer thus translates it: "Let each one of you lay aside by himself." Dr. Justin Edwards, in his Family Testament of the American Tract Society, p. 286, thus gives it: "Lay by himself in store; at home; that there be no gatherings; that their gifts might be ready when the apostle should come." Surely all these authorities, and others which might be cited, are sufficient to settle the question beyond all controversy, that there is no public collection intended, but on the contrary that the act required was to be done at home.

Again, the act required is not such an one as would be consistent with Sabbath sacredness. They were to lay by them on the first day of the week as God had prospered them. To tell how God had prospered them during the week past, if a business man, would necessitate the reckoning of accounts. Our first-day friends would hardly relish the idea of finding some of their church members who were merchants, busy reckoning up columns of figures to ascertain their amount of prosperity during the past week, on what they call the "Christian Sabbath." Yet this is precisely what this command of the great apostle to "lay by him in store, as God had prospered him" would necessitate in the case of any one who had large business transactions.

Here we see the same fact stated which has been apparent in the other cases where the first day of the week is mentioned. Secular labor is spoken of as being done on that day; and in this last instance the apostle required it. Surely this is not consistent with Sabbath holiness. We therefore conclude that this last mention of the first day utterly fails to prove the practice of holding religious meetings on the first day of the week in the apostolic age, and fails to give the slightest sanction to any claim of sacredness.

We next notice references made to the Bible Sabbath during the days of the apostles. "But when they departed from Perga, they came to Antioch in Pisidia, and went into the synagogue on the Sabbath day, and sat down." Acts 13:14. After this Paul gave a masterly discourse to those assembled, proving that Jesus is the Christ. We learn from this scripture that the day St. Luke calls the Sabbath some twelve years after, which many claim had been changed, was still the seventh day, the very day when the Jews met in their synagogues. At the close of this discourse, we read: "And when the Jews were gone out of the synagogue, the Gentiles besought that these words might be preached to them the next Sabbath." "And the next Sabbath day came almost the whole city together to hear the word of God." Acts 13:42, 44. Here again the inspired word of God positively declares that the seventh day, on which the Jews met in their synagogues, *was the Sabbath day* in the year A. D. 45.

We are well aware how first-day advocates try to avoid the force of this argument by saying, "It was the Jewish Sabbath, of course," and "the apostles went into the synagogue to preach, simply because they could not get opportunity to speak to the Jews any other day," and "the apostles did not hold religious meetings with the Gentiles on the Jewish Sabbath," etc. But the very fact that they in every case place the word "Jewish" before the word "Sabbath," when speaking of the seventh day of the week, as a term of reproach, while they speak of the first day of the week as *the Sabbath*, without any such qualifying phrase, shows the sense in which they speak of that day, as distinguished from the manner in which inspired men speak of it many years this side of the cross. Why did not St. Luke speak of the day as the "Jewish Sabbath," if his practice then was the same as that of many Christian ministers now? We could not persuade these estimable men to speak of the seventh day as *the Sabbath day* before their congregations in public. They never do it. They would feel at once that all who heard them would draw the conclusion that they considered it a sacred day, should they do so. The observers of the seventh day always call it "the Sabbath day," because they regard it as such.

How shall we explain the fact that St. Luke, whenever he has occasion to speak of it, always calls it by the same name that its modern observers do, and never calls it the Jewish Sabbath, except on the supposition that he observed it himself, and considered no other day of the week the Sabbath day? This writer is a Christian, writing for the Christian dispensation. He calls those institutions which he names, what they really are. He always calls the seventh day, when he has occasion to speak of it, "the Sabbath," just as writers had been doing for four thousand years, showing that no change had occurred. He never in a single instance calls the first day of the week by any such title, or by any sacred title whatever; yet many good people believe that he had been keeping the first day of the week as the Sabbath for thirty years, and not keeping the seventh day as such. We leave it for first-day observers to explain such inconsistency.

We next notice the claim that the apostles did not hold meetings on the seventh-day Sabbath, except with the Jews, for the sake of reaching them. Acts 13:42 implies that this meeting on the first Sabbath mentioned, was a mixed meeting of Jews and Gentiles; for the latter requested that these words might be repeated to them on the next Sabbath. This shows at least that they were somewhat conversant with the discourse. What an excellent opportunity this presented to the apostle to inform them of the first-day Sabbath, if there had been any instituted! How readily our modern ministers would have remarked, "You need not wait a whole week; to-morrow is the Christian's Sabbath, the day in which we instruct the Gentiles." But not a word of this do we find. They waited a whole week; then nearly the whole city turned out to hear the gospel. Luke says it was "the next Sabbath day" when this great gathering occurred. It was evidently a week later than the other meeting. If it was the *next* Sabbath day, then most certainly Sunday was *not* a Sabbath day. Here was a *Gentile meeting* on the Sabbath day, and no one can truthfully deny it. Here we have two consecutive Sabbath days in which the great apostle held religious services, instructing far more Gentiles than Jews.

We next notice Acts 16:13: "And on the Sabbath we went out of the city by a river side, where prayer was wont to be made; and we sat down and spake unto the women which resorted thither." Here we have another religious meeting of the apostle to the Gentiles, in the Gentile city of Philippi, on the seventh-day Sabbath. As the Greek language puts it, it was "*the Sabbath day*," so called by a Christian writer.

"Now when they had passed through Amphipolis and Apollonia, they came to Thessalonica, where was a synagogue of the Jews. And Paul, as his manner was, went in unto them, and three Sabbath days reasoned with them out of the Scriptures." Acts 17:1, 2. Twenty years after the resurrection, we here have another instance, in a Gentile city, of Paul's using the ancient Sabbath as a day for religious meetings, and of Luke's declaring to the Christian world that the day in which the Jews met in their synagogues was still the Sabbath day of holy writ. Another very significant remark made by the historian is that it was "Paul's manner" thus to use the Sabbath day for religious teaching. In this respect he followed Christ's example perfectly. The same writer declares that it was our Saviour's "custom" to do the same thing. Luke 4:16. All agree that our Lord in doing this was keeping the Sabbath commandment, and showing proper respect for the worship of God on that day. The Sabbath was ordained for that purpose, as a day for religious worship. It would be impossible to show a particle of difference between Paul's "manner" of treating the Sabbath and Christ's "custom." They pursued the same course toward the Sabbath, because their relation to Jehovah's rest day was just the same. It was the day appointed for religious instruction. It was obligatory in both cases.

Another very significant point in connection with this text of scripture, is the fact that here we have an account of the origin of the Thessalonian church, to which Paul addressed one of his epistles. We cannot question but what the members of this church were observers of the seventh-day Sabbath. Paul, in his letter to them, uses this language: "For ye, brethren, became followers of the churches of God, which in Judea are in Christ Jesus." 1 Thess. 2:14. "And ye became followers of us, and of the Lord, having received the word in much affliction, with joy of the Holy Ghost, so that ye were ensamples to all that believe in Macedonia and Achaia." 1 Thess. 1:6, 7. Paul, we know, was an observer of the Sabbath; so also was our Saviour. Jesus himself declares, "I have kept my Father's commandments." The Sabbath command was one of these.

St. Paul, when he arrived in Rome, A. D. 62, called the "chief of the Jews together," and said unto them, "I have committed nothing against the people, or customs of our fathers." Acts 28:17. None will deny that the observance of the Sabbath was one of these "customs." Hence we are forced to conclude that Paul kept the Sabbath. These Thessalonian brethren followed Paul and Christ; therefore they also were observers of the Sabbath. The brethren of Macedonia and Achaia followed the same example. The churches of Judea even, according to the admission of many first-day commentators, still kept the Sabbath. We see, therefore, that the early Gentile Christians imitated them in this practice. We note, also, this fact, which is brought to view in the text we are considering: here were three more Sabbath days in which Paul held religious meetings, making six, with the three previously mentioned.

We next notice Paul's visit to Corinth. "And he reasoned in the synagogue every Sabbath, and persuaded the Jews and the Greeks. . . . And he continued there a year and six months, teaching the word of God among them." Acts 18:4, 11. Paul met for a portion of the time in the synagogue; but after the Jews "opposed," he continued to teach the people in the house of Justus, "whose house joined hard to the synagogue." The record states that he reasoned in the synagogue, teaching Gentiles as well as Jews "every Sabbath," and that he continued in the synagogue and the house which "joined hard to" it, a year and six months. There would be seventy-eight Sabbaths in that period. These, with the six previously noted, would make some eighty-four Sabbaths in which Luke records the fact of Paul's holding meetings in Gentile cities with both "Jews and Greeks." Paul was the great apostle to the Gentiles; and all these instances of Sabbath meetings mentioned, occurred in Gentile cities and not in Judea. Is not this significant? It would have been much more easy to explain away, if it had been in the Jews' own country where all these meetings on the Sabbath occurred. We find no instances in which any secular work whatever occurred in connection with any of these Sabbath meetings,—no long journeys traveled, or reckoning of accounts.

Sunday observers cite Paul's night meeting in Acts 20, and dwell upon it with much satisfaction. Yet he and his companions used the light part of that day for ordinary secular business. One night meeting they consider strong evidence for first-day sacredness; yet that very instance really counts more for the Sabbath than for the first day; for the disciples remained there over the Sabbath, and as soon as the light of the first day dawned, they started on their long journey toward Jerusalem. They did not start on the Sabbath, but they did on Sunday. Doubtless the reason why that night meeting was mentioned, was the most remarkable occurrence of raising the dead man Eutychus. This was one of the greatest miracles that Paul ever wrought.

But here we have scores of religious meetings on a day which Inspiration declares to be the Sabbath, in which Jews and Gentiles are instructed in the truths of the gospel; and yet men teach that it was not the Sabbath day, but the first day, which is never in a single instance called the Sabbath. So hard is it to see a truth which involves a cross.

We next notice a text which is claimed by first-day observers as evidence in behalf of Sunday, but which we claim affords excellent proof in behalf of the Lord's holy Sabbath. "I was in the Spirit on the Lord's day, and heard behind me a great voice, as of a trumpet." Rev. 1:10. This language is supposed to have been written in the year A. D. 96, sixty-five years after the resurrection of Christ. It is claimed that by the term "Lord's day" is meant the first day of the week, the day on which our Saviour rose from the dead. But the very point to be proved is assumed. We want evidence of a substantial character that the first day of the week *is* the "Lord's day." Not a hint from the Scriptures is ever cited to prove this important point. No sacred writer ever calls it such. In every case where it is mentioned, as we have seen in eight instances, it has the same secular title. St. John himself, in writing his Gospel, some two or three years later than the book of Revelation was written, as is generally supposed, calls it twice "the first day of the week." John 20:1, 19. If he had intended the first day of the week to be understood by the term "Lord's day," why did he not call it so still later when he wrote his Gospel?

No good reason can be assigned for calling it the Lord's day. The Lord never intimated any more regard for it than for any other secular day. The fact that he rose from the dead on it does not entitle it to any higher regard from us than the sixth day, the day of his crucifixion, the one on which our salvation was purchased by his spilt blood; or Thursday, the day on which he ascended, to become our high priest. Not one well-authenticated instance can be found where Sunday was ever called the Lord's day before the year A. D. 194, just about one hundred years later than the time when this was written by St. John,—a point where Christianity had become much corrupted.

We confidently claim that this "Lord's day" is God's holy Sabbath day. For four thousand years it had been constantly recognized as a day peculiarly sacred to the Lord. He rested upon it, and set it apart to a holy use, placing his blessing upon it. Gen. 2:3. In the law of God he said, "Remember the Sabbath day to keep it holy. . . . The seventh day is the Sabbath of the Lord thy God. . . . The Lord blessed the Sabbath day, and hallowed it." Ex. 20:8–11. The prophet says, "If thou turn away thy foot from *the Sabbath*, from doing thy pleasure on *my holy day*." Isa. 58:13. Surely this language unmistakably identifies which day is "the Lord's day." It can be none other than the one he has always claimed.

But it is sometimes objected that in the original Greek, the term "Lord" used in the text refers to Christ, and not to God the Father; that it is not Jehovah's day, but a special day which Christ claims as his own. Very well; of what day does Christ claim to be the Lord?—"The Son of man is Lord also of the Sabbath." Mark 2:28. Is not the day of which Christ says he is Lord *the Lord's day?* So we believe. Does he anywhere say he is Lord of the first day of the week?— Not a text is ever quoted by any one to show it. We therefore conclude that the day on which St. John had this heavenly vision was the Lord's holy Sabbath. Let it be noticed by all that at the very close of the first century of the Christian era, the Lord has a day which he still calls his own, which we have shown to be the holy Sabbath. All days, then, are not alike. God claims at the very close of the canon of inspiration, in the book of Revelation, as he did at its beginning, in the book of Genesis, that one day is his own.

We will quote one text more concerning the time the holy Sabbath will continue, with which to close the Biblical argument of this question: "For as the new heavens and the new earth, which I will make, shall remain before me, saith the Lord, so shall your seed and your name remain. And it shall come to pass, that from one new moon to another, and from one Sabbath to another, shall all flesh come to worship before me, saith the Lord." Isa. 66:22, 23. The new heavens and the new earth are created a thousand years after the coming of Christ. 2 Peter 3:

8-13 ; Rev. 20 : 4-15 ; 21 : 1. The new earth will be the abode of the saved to all eternity. The holy city, the new Jerusalem, will be in it, and there, also, will be the tree of life, bearing its twelve manner of fruits monthly. Rev. 22 : 2. To this blessed metropolis of the new creation will the saints of God come each month, to partake of its fruits, and each week, on the holy Sabbath, to worship God.

That blessed day which God set apart at creation to serve as a beautiful memorial of the works of the Creator, will be still more gladly kept when sin and the curse have been forever abolished. Why should not this blessed institution ever exist as a reminder of the glory of God in creation? Nothing could be more fitting. The word of God positively declares that the holy Sabbath—that Sabbath with which the prophet Isaiah was well acquainted—will be kept in the reign of the new heavens and the new earth. What, then, is the conclusion which the Scriptures compel us to make in reference to the continuance of the Bible Sabbath? The great majority of Christians admit that for four thousand years the seventh day was the only weekly Sabbath. Here we find the same day being kept in Eden restored, continuing to all eternity. Can we suppose that an intermission of about two thousand years occurred between these two eternities? and that another Sabbath was set up to take the place of this great memorial of the work of Christ and Jehovah, which God has ordained to be kept in the eternal world? Can we think such an event probable? Such a conclusion would be unphilosophical, absurd, preposterous.

The prophet of God in holy vision beholds the Sabbath of the Lord carried far beyond this world of sin. Thus the Holy Scriptures place the seventh-day Sabbath like a grand arch at the beginning of the race of man, spanning the six thousand years of human probation, and reaching into a renovated world after sin is forever destroyed. No place is left for another weekly Sabbath to come in. Few realize the vast importance of the Sabbatic institution. It is the golden clasp which binds man to his Maker. It keeps in memory the true God as the creator of all things. Had man ever observed it in the true spirit, idolatry could never have had an existence.

CHAPTER X.

THE TWO REST DAYS IN SECULAR HISTORY.

IN the consideration of the Sabbath and its supposed change, we have now reached an important point. We have had, hitherto, the inspired, unerring word of the Lord as our text-book of authority; and we need not discount a single statement it has made on the subject under investigation. We have found the Sabbath of the Lord still standing with undiminished obligation, at the close of the canon of inspiration, and at the end of the first century of the Christian era. Now we enter upon a very different order of things. We know that a change of the Sabbath has been attempted, for the majority of professed Christians are found observing the first day of the week and not the seventh. As no account of a change is to be found in the Bible, we must look for it this side of the close of the first century.

The authorities to which we must now look will be the so-called "Christian Fathers," ecclesiastical historians, the decrees of emperors, and the decisions of councils. We shall find much of fable, contradictory statements, unreliable traditions, and doctrines never taught in the Bible. In the second, third, and fourth centuries, great changes came into the church. It ceased to be the humble, pure church of Christ and the apostles, but became rather a worldly, popular church, paying more heed to ambition, vain show, the love of supremacy, the traditions of men, and heathen notions, than to the word of God. The great errors which finally culminated in the full development of the Catholic Church, here had their rise.

It is not the design of this comparatively brief treatise to notice all the points and questions raised on the subject of the Sabbath and its change, by the multitude of authors and authorities who have discussed this subject. The "History of the Sabbath," by Eld. J. N. Andrews, published by the *Review and Herald* Office, Battle Creek, Mich., does this in a most thorough and conclusive manner; and all who desire to see every argument raised by first-day authors fully considered, should certainly secure this book. It is a work of great thoroughness, comprising 548 pages.

Our object in this treatise is to present, in as brief a manner as possible, a connected view of the attempted change of the day, and the authority for it. The authorities we quote will, in almost every case, be those who kept the first day of the week for the Sabbath, as far as they kept any day, and not those who favored the seventh day.

Let us briefly notice some predictions of the Scriptures concerning this period upon which we are now entering, as well as the statements of leading Protestant authors concerning the character of these early times. "For I know this, that after my departing shall grievous wolves enter in among you, not sparing the flock. Also of your own selves shall men arise, speaking perverse things, to draw away disciples after them." Acts 20 : 29, 30. "For the time will come when they will not endure sound doctrine; but after their own lusts shall they heap to themselves teachers, having itching ears; and they shall turn away their ears from the truth, and shall be turned unto fables." 2 Tim. 4 : 3, 4. "Let no man deceive you by any means, for that day shall not come, except there come a falling away [literal Greek, apostasy] first, and that man of sin be revealed, the son of perdition, who opposeth and exalteth himself above all that is called God, or that is worshiped ; so that he as God sitteth in the temple of God, showing himself that he is God. . . . For the mystery of iniquity doth already work ; only he who now letteth [hindereth] will let, until he be taken out of the way. And then shall that Wicked be revealed, whom the

Lord shall consume with the spirit of his mouth, and shall destroy with the brightness of his coming." 2 Thess. 2 : 3, 4, 7, 8.

These scriptures are very explicit in predicting a great apostasy in the church, the beginning of which was already existing in Paul's day. It is not enough, therefore, to trace a doctrine or practice back almost or even quite to the days of the apostles; for great errors had their rise in that very period. The real question is, Does such a doctrine owe its origin to the Bible? The Roman Catholic Church holds many doctrines which are very ancient, and yet are wholly contrary to the Bible. The prophet Daniel foretells the rise of a power which should undertake great changes even in the law of God. "And he shall speak great words against the Most High, and shall wear out the saints of the Most High, and think to change times and laws [the times and the law, *Revised Version*]; and they shall be given into his hand until a time and times and the dividing of time." Dan. 7 : 25. The best commentators agree that the Catholic power is here intended. The fourth beast mentioned in the vision of the seventh chapter of this book, is said to be the "fourth kingdom." Verse 23. This was certainly the Roman kingdom. Rome under the popes was more marvelous than Rome under the Cæsars. This power was to "think to change" the times and the law of God. This expression clearly refers to the Sabbath of God's law. Will history bear out this prediction?

According to the best Protestant authors,

what was the character of the religious changes occurring during the second and third centuries, and what credence should we give to the so-called Christian Fathers?

"From Adrian [A. D. 117] to Justinian, . . . few institutions, either human or divine, were permitted to stand on their former basis."—*Gibbon's Decline and Fall of the Roman Empire*, chap. 44, par. 7.

Says Robinson, the Baptist historian:—

"Toward the latter end of the second century, most of the churches assumed a new form, the first simplicity disappeared, and insensibly, as the old disciples retired to their graves, their children, along with new converts, both Jews and Gentiles, came forward and new-modeled the cause."—*Eccl. Researches*, chap. 6, p. 51. Ed. 1792.

Says Mr. Bower, in his "History of the Popes":—

"To avoid being imposed upon, we ought to treat tradition as we do a notorious . . liar, to whom we give no credit unless what he says is confirmed to us by some person of undoubted veracity. . . . False and lying traditions are of an early date, and the greatest men have, out of a pious credulity, suffered themselves to be imposed upon by them."—Vol. 1, p. 1, Phila. Ed. 1847.

Dr. Adam Clarke uses the following language concerning the Fathers:—

"We should take heed how we quote the Fathers in proof of the doctrines of the gospel, because he who knows them best, knows that on many of those subjects they blow hot and cold."—*Autobiography of Adam Clarke*, p. 134.

Martin Luther says:—

"When God's word is by the *Fathers* expounded, constructed, and glossed, then in my judgment it is even like unto one that straineth milk through a coal sack, which must needs spoil the milk and make it black.

Even so, likewise, God's word of itself is sufficiently pure, clean, bright, and clear; but through the doctrines, books, and writings of the Fathers, it is very surely darkened, falsified, and spoiled."—*Table Talk*, p. 228.

Says Du Pin, one of the most celebrated and reliable of the Catholic historians:—

"It is a surprising thing to consider how many spurious books we find in antiquity, nay, even in the first ages of the church."

Dr. Clarke says again of the Fathers, in his comments on Proverbs 8:—

"But of these we may safely state that there is not a truth in the most orthodox creed that cannot be proved by their authority, nor a heresy that has disgraced the Romish Church, that may not challenge them as its abettors. In points of doctrine, *their authority is, with me, nothing. The word of God alone contains my creed.*"

We could multiply statements of this kind from eminent authors almost *ad infinitum*. We have introduced them simply to show how unreliable for authority on religious duties these Fathers are, and what an age of corruption was that portion of the historical field we are considering. Our only safety is to take the Bible alone as authority in matters of religion. By it Paul says the man of God may be "thoroughly furnished unto all *good* works."

It is in such an age as this, and from such authorities as these Fathers, that the principal evidence of a change of the Sabbath is derived. The ante-Nicæan Fathers are those Christian writers who flourished after the time of the apostles and before the Council of Nicæa, A. D. 325. As we have seen, the best of authorities, like Dr. Clarke, declare that the Fathers sustain the heresies of the Roman Church, as well as many of the essential truths of the gospel. In short, they lived in that age of transition from the pure truths of the word of God to that great system of corruption which developed into Roman Catholicism.

To bring briefly before the reader a comprehensive statement relative to the bearing of the Fathers upon the subject of the change of the Sabbath, we quote from Andrews's "History of the Sabbath," pp. 206, 207 :—

"But next to the deception under which men fall when they are made to believe that the Bible may be corrected by the Fathers, is the deception practiced upon them as to what the Fathers actually teach. It is asserted that the Fathers bear explicit testimony to the change of the Sabbath by Christ as a historical fact, and that they knew that this was so because they had conversed with the apostles, or with some who had conversed with them. It is also asserted that the Fathers called the first day of the week the Christian Sabbath, and that they refrained from labor on that day as an act of obedience to the fourth commandment.

"Now it is a most remarkable fact that every one of these assertions is false. The people who trust in the Fathers as their authority for departing from God's commandment, are miserably deceived as to what the Fathers teach.

"1. The Fathers are so far from testifying that the apostles told them Christ changed the Sabbath, that not even one of them ever alludes to such a change.

"2. No one of them ever calls the first day the Christian Sabbath, nor, indeed, ever calls it a Sabbath of any kind.

"3. They never represent it as a day on which ordinary labor was sinful; nor do they represent the observance of Sunday as an act of obedience to the fourth commandment.

"4. The modern doctrine of the change of the Sabbath was therefore absolutely unknown in the first centuries of the Christian Church."

We are now prepared to notice the steps by which the Sabbath gradually lost its position of eminence, and also how the first day of the week gradually usurped its place.

CHAPTER XI.

THE SABBATH OBSERVED FOR SEVERAL CENTURIES AFTER CHRIST.

WE shall now show from the testimony of those who observed the first day of the week, as far as they observed any day as a Sabbath, that the seventh day continued to be kept for several centuries after Christ, but with a sacredness gradually decreasing in proportion to the rising influence of Sunday, until the Roman Catholic Church became so powerful that, wherever it had sway, it put down the Sabbath and exalted the first day of the week to its place in the observance of the people. This, as we shall see, was a gradual work, taking several centuries for its accomplishment.

Says the learned Mr. Morer, of the Church of England:—

"The primitive Christians had a great veneration for the Sabbath, and spent the day in devotion and sermons. And it is not to be doubted but that they derived this practice from the apostles themselves, as appears by several scriptures to that purpose."— *Dialogues on the Lord's Day*, p. 189.

A learned English writer of the seventeenth century, William Twisse, D. D., thus states the early history of these two days:—

"Yet for some hundred years in the primitive church, not the Lord's day only, but the seventh day also, was religiously observed, not by Ebion and Cerinthus alone, but by the pious Christians also, as Baronius writeth and Gomarus confesseth, and Rivet also, that we are bound in conscience, under the gospel, to allow for God's service a better proportion of time than the Jews did under the law, rather than a worse."— *Morality of the Fourth Commandment*, p. 9, London, 1641.

The learned Giesler also states the same fact, and that this practice of observing the seventh day was not confined to the Jewish converts:—

"While the Jewish Christians of Palestine retained the entire Mosaic law, and consequently the Jewish festivals, the Gentile Christians observed also the Sabbath and the passover, with reference to the last scenes of Jesus' life, but without Jewish superstition."— *Eccl. Hist.*, Vol. 1, chap. 2, sec. 30.

These statements are certainly very explicit as proof of the continued observance of the Sabbath in the centuries immediately succeeding the apostolic age, and these evidences come from those who could have no prejudice in favor of the seventh day.

But we notice others of similar import. Coleman speaks as follows: —

"The last day of the week was strictly kept in connection with that of the first day for a long time after the overthrow of the temple and its worship. Down even to the fifth century the observance of the Jewish Sabbath was continued in the Christian church, but with a rigor and solemnity diminishing until it was wholly discontinued." — *Ancient Christianity Exemplified*, chap. 26, sec. 2.

In the above extract, this writer speaks of the first day's being observed also. In subsequent language he tells us how it was regarded in these early ages: —

"During the early ages of the church it was never entitled 'the Sabbath,' this word being confined to the seventh day of the week, the Jewish Sabbath, which, as we have already said, continued to be observed for several centuries by the converts to Christianity." — *Anc. Christ. Exem.*, chap. 26, sec. 2.

He tells us again in a few words how the first day of the week, which he, like many other first-day writers calls "the Lord's day," though without good authority for so doing, came gradually to work its way into the position of the true Sabbath: —

"The observance of the Lord's day was ordered while yet the Sabbath of the Jews was continued; nor was the latter superseded until the former had acquired the same solemnity and importance which belonged, at first, to that great day which God originally ordained and blessed. . . . But in time, after the Lord's day was fully established, the observance of the Sabbath of the Jews was gradually discontinued and was finally denounced as heretical." — *Idem.*

We shall see that the facts of history fully sustain the statement of this first-day writer. The Sunday festival at first only asked toleration; but as it gradually gained strength, it undermined the Sabbath, and finally its adherents denounced its observance as heretical.

Bishop Jeremy Taylor, of the Church of England, a man of great learning, also bears testimony incidentally to the same fact, — the observance of the Sabbath for centuries after Christ, — though he was a decided opponent of Sabbatic obligation : —

"It [the Lord's day] was not introduced by virtue of the fourth commandment, because they for almost three hundred years together kept that day which was in that commandment." — *Ductor Dubitantium,* part 1, book 2, chap. 2, rule 6, sec. 51.

We quote another testimony from a member of the English Church, Edward Brerewood, professor in Gresham College, London : —

"The ancient Sabbath did remain and was observed, together with the celebration of the Lord's day, by the Christians of the East Church, above three hundred years after our Saviour's death; and besides that, no other day for more hundreds of years than I spake of before, was known in the church by the name of the Sabbath but that." — *Learned Treatise of the Sabbath,* p. 77, Oxford, 1631.

These testimonies should certainly satisfy reasonable minds of the continued observance of the Sabbath of the Lord for a long time after the death of the apostles. As will be shown when we consider the growth of the Sunday institution, it gradually increased from several causes, till it became a rival of the ancient day. By the end of the third century it had acquired almost an equality with the Sabbath itself in the regard of many of the Gentile Christians. In the same ratio, the latter was decreasing in relative importance in the minds of many.

In the beginning of the fourth century an event occurred which vastly accelerated this process, and raised the first day and correspondingly depressed the seventh day in the balancing scale of esteem in the minds of the people. This was an edict of the emperor Constantine, issued A. D. 321, which required all trades-people and towns-people to rest on "the venerable day of the sun," though it did not forbid labor in sowing and planting in the country. This is the first law commanding rest on the first day of the week, which can be found on record in all history, either human or sacred. We shall fully consider it when we notice the steps by which the first day rose to authority. The effect of this law upon the ancient Sabbath was greatly to decrease the regard of the people for it, and to turn the tide of influence strongly in favor of its rival.

On this point an able writer, Mr. Cox, remarks : —

> "Very shortly after the period when Constantine issued his edict enjoining the general observance of Sunday throughout the Roman empire, the party that had contended for the observance of the seventh day, dwindled into insignificance. The observance of Sunday as a public festival, during which all business, with the exception of rural employments, was intermitted, came to be more and more generally established ever after this time, throughout both the Greek and Latin churches. There is no evidence, however, that either in this, or at a period much later, the observance was viewed as deriving any obligation from the fourth commandment ; it seems to have been regarded as an institution corresponding in nature with Christmas, Good Friday, and other festivals of the church; and as resting with them on the ground of ecclesiastical authority and tradition."— *Sabbath Laws Examined*, pp. 280, 281.

However, even with this powerful influence of the great Roman emperor thrown into the scale against the ancient Sabbath, it still continued to share public esteem for a long time. It took a strong combination of influences, secular and religious, entirely to obliterate from the public memory this grand ancient institution, the Sabbath of creation ; but the gradual disintegrating influences continued to wear away its God-given sanctity. A heathen Roman emperor, a tyrant, a murderer, one who killed his own wife and his own son and many other innocent persons, took one prominent step to debase it. The Sabbath never fully recovered from this blow, although it was still regarded as a day for religious meetings. Dr. Heylyn, speaking of the Sabbath in Constantine's time, says : —

> "As for the Saturday, that retained its wonted credit in the Eastern churches, little inferior to the Lord's day, if not plainly equal; not as the Sabbath, think not so; but as a day designed unto sacred meetings."— *History of the Sabbath*, part 2, chap. 3, sec. 5.

After Constantine's time, there seems to have been in a measure a revival of interest in, and reverence for, the Sabbath in the minds of many Christians, at least in the Eastern churches, where the influence of the Roman Church was less powerful.

Prof. Stuart, in speaking of the period from Constantine to the Council of Laodicea, A. D. 364, says : —

> "The practice of it [the keeping of the Sabbath] was continued by Christians who were jealous for the honor of the Mosaic law, and finally became, as we have seen, predominant throughout Christendom. It was supposed at length that the fourth commandment did require the observance of the seventh-day Sabbath (not merely a seventh part of time); and reasoning as Christians of the present day are wont to do, viz., that *all* which belonged to the ten commandments was immutable and perpetual, the churches in general came gradually to regard the seventh-day Sabbath as altogether sacred." — *Appendix to Gurney's History, etc., of the Sabbath*, pp. 115, 116.

The church had by this time become greatly corrupted. When Constantine professed Christianity, it became the popular religion. In order to serve in the army or in the courts, or hold any official position, men had to profess to be Christians ; and Gibbon declares that many did this, but continued to worship their idols in secret. Vast numbers joined the church. The bishops sought high positions, wealth, and place, dressing in gorgeous attire, and there was very little resemblance indeed between religion then and in the days of persecution. What did this great Catholic Church now do, when they saw the Sabbath once more gaining some of its former sanctity, and an interest in it reviving ?—They held a great council at Laodicea, and, among other things, passed a decree that Christians should *not rest on the seventh-day Sabbath*, and *pronounced a curse upon all who should do so.* We present the following statements of eminent authors on this point :—

Mr. James, in addressing the University of Oxford, used this language :—

"When the practice of keeping Saturday Sabbaths, which had become so general at the close of this century, was evidently gaining ground in the Eastern church, a decree was passed in the council held in Laodicea [A. D. 364], 'that members of the church should not rest from work on the Sabbath day, like Jews, but should labor on that day, and preferring in honor the Lord's day ; then, if it be in their power, should rest from work as Christians.'"—*Sermons on the Sacraments and Sabbath*, pp. 122, 123.

Prynne thus testifies :—

"It is certain that Christ himself, his apostles, and the primitive Christians for some good space of time, did constantly observe the seventh-day Sabbath, . . . the Evangelists and St. Luke in the Acts ever styling it the

Sabbath day, . . . and making mention of its . . . solemnization by the apostles and other Christians, . . . it being still solemnized by many Christians after the apostles' times, even till the Council of Laodicea, as ecclesiastical writers and the twenty-ninth canon of that council testify, which runs thus: 'Because Christians ought not to Judaize and to rest in the Sabbath, but to work in that day (which many did refuse at that time to do). But preferring in honor the Lord's day (there being then a great controversy among Christians which of these two days . . . should have precedency), if they should desired to rest they should do this as Christians. Wherefore if they shall be found to Judaize, let them be accursed from Christ.' . . . The seventh-day Sabbath was . . . solemnized by Christ, the apostles, and primitive Christians, till the Laodicean Council did in a manner quite abolish the observation of it. . . . The Council of Laodicea . . . first settled the observation of the Lord's day, and prohibited . . . the keeping of the Jewish Sabbath under an anathema."—*Dissertation on the Lord's Day Sabbath*, pp. 33, 34, 44. Edition 1633.

We also quote from an old English writer, John Ley :—

"From the apostle's time until the Council of Laodicea, which was about the year 364, the holy observation of the Jews' Sabbath continued, as may be proved out of many authors; yea, notwithstanding the decree of that council against it."—*Sunday a Sabbath*, p. 163. Edition 1640.

From this time onward the general disregard of the ancient Sabbath was a foregone conclusion. It did continue, as we shall show, in some localities where the Catholic Church had not the power to abolish it. But the influence of that church was so great, its jurisdiction so extensive, its hatred to the Sabbath of the Lord so bitter, and its efforts in behalf of the Sunday Sabbath so active, that for centuries the ancient Sabbath made but little figure among Christian communities. We charge plainly and squarely upon the corruptions of that Christianity which developed into the Roman Catholic Church, the change of the Sabbath, and the abolition of the ancient Sabbath of the Lord, contrary to the practice of the church of Jesus Christ. The influences which hastened this result dwelt in Rome itself in a special sense, far more than in other sections. The bishops of Rome manifested their enmity against the Sabbath far more than those of any other city.

About the year A. D. 200, the Church of Rome turned the Sabbath into a fast day, evidently to make the Sabbath disreputable. Says Mr. James, before the University of Oxford :—

"The Western church began to fast on Saturday at the beginning of the third century."

Dr. Charles Hase, of Germany, says :—

"The Roman Church regarded Saturday as a fast day in direct opposition to those who regarded it as a Sabbath. Sunday remained a joyful festival," etc.—*Ancient Church History*, part 1, div. 2, A. D. 100–312, sec. 69.

Says the great German historian, Neander :—

"In the Western churches, particularly the Roman, where opposition to Judaism was the prevailing tendency, this very opposition produced the custom of celebrating the Saturday in particular as a fast day."—*Neander*, p. 186.

By Judaism is doubtless meant the observance of the Sabbath. Fasting is never popular, and of course, seeing the Sunday was made as joyful a day as possible, the Sabbath was disliked. The Eastern churches did not follow in this practice of fasting on the Sabbath for a long time, and censured the Roman Church for doing it.

The Roman Church made the first edict in behalf of Sunday. It required the observance of the passover on the Sunday following Good Friday, while the great majority of the other churches celebrated it on the fourteenth day of the first month, no matter what day of the week this might be. Victor, bishop of Rome, in the year 196, tried to impose this upon all the churches; that is, to compel them to observe it on Sunday. Dowling calls it the "earliest instance of Romish assumption." The churches of Asia Minor would not comply with his wishes. Bower says that upon receipt of their letter saying this, Victor, giving way "to an impotent and ungovernable passion, published bitter invectives against all the churches of Asia," etc.—*History of the Popes, under Victor*.

Constantine's edict in behalf of the "venerable day of the sun" went forth backed by the whole influence of Rome, where, indeed, it had its source. At the Council at Nicæa, A. D. 325, through the powerful influence of Constantine, the position of the Roman Church concerning the celebration of the passover on Sunday, was carried through. Thus Rome secured a victory in behalf of Sunday. One special reason urged by the emperor in behalf of Sunday was this: "Let us, then, have nothing in common with the most hostile rabble of the Jews." This hatred of the Jews was one of the strongest causes why the Sabbath was suppressed. Sylvester, bishop of Rome at this time, and Eusebius, the historian, were special favorites of the emperor, and doubtless used their utmost influence with him to bring about these results.

We see, therefore, the Roman influence in all these moves to suppress the Sabbath. They culminated in the Council of Laodicea, A. D. 364, when the keeping of the Sabbath was denounced, and those who observed it were placed under a curse. Who can fail to see the leading spirit in this movement? Whenever the Roman Church has had authority, the Sabbath has been degraded. It continued much longer in the Eastern churches than in the Western, where the Roman influence was paramount. After the removal of the capital city from Rome to Constantinople by the Emperor Constantine, there was quite a struggle on the part of the bishop of the latter city for the mastery; but to no purpose, though it finally resulted in the separation of the Roman and Greek Catholic churches. But throughout the Western churches the adherents of the Sabbath had little favor; though we find here and there traces of Sabbath-keepers in retired places all through the Dark Ages. Of these we will speak hereafter.

Thus we see that the Roman Catholic Church, with the pope at its head, "exalted" itself "above God" by setting aside his law. Thus he fulfilled the prophet's prediction, "He shall think to change the times and the law."

CHAPTER XII.

STEPS BY WHICH SUNDAY ROSE INTO PROMINENCE.

IN this treatise, giving an account of the change of the Sabbath from the seventh to the first day of the week, it is but reasonable that we should present the prominent causes which led to this result. We have shown that the Bible gives no account of such a change; but it has been made, and the great mass of Christians are now observing the first day of the week. There must have been the united action of powerful causes to accomplish this. We present, as the most prominent of these, the following:—

1. Sunday was an ancient heathen festival, which, from time immemorial, had been looked upon with favor, and regarded as more or less sacred by worshipers of the sun; so that when Christianity made progress among the idolatrous Gentile nations, it came in conflict with this custom.

2. The difficulty of keeping the seventh-day Sabbath, surrounded as Christians were by the great masses of the people who did not observe it, but who paid more or less respect to Sunday.

3. The voluntary observance of memorable days, such as the day of the crucifixion, the resurrection, the ascension, etc., as the church lost its purity, and began to wander away from the Scriptures.

4. Hatred of the Jews, which was cherished among the Gentile nations, especially the Roman people, and after the death of the apostles, among Christians, on account of the persecutions they received, and because the Jews put Christ to death.

5. Especially, as the work of apostasy proceeded, the acceptance of tradition in place of the Bible. Here the church lost its connection with God, and wandered into heathenish practices, setting aside precious truths of divine authority, and accepting the inventions of men.

6. The hatred of the church of Rome to the Sabbath of the Lord, seeking constantly to lower it in the estimation of the people, and to exalt the first day in its place. When this church came fully into power, it accomplished the work.

These influences combined, in the space of centuries, gradually to undermine the Sabbath, and to exalt the first day of the week in popular estimation, till, in the observance of the masses, it wholly superseded the Sabbath. We will notice more particularly some of these causes.

The festival of Sunday is very ancient, reaching back into hoary antiquity. No person can tell where or when it did originate. It was of idolatrous origin, and was consecrated to the worship of the sun. There was a time, in the days of the early patriarchs, when the worship of the true God was universal. But Satan, the great enemy of God, instituted idolatry. The worship of the sun, moon, and stars, especially the former, was the most ancient and prevalent form of idolatry. Under various names, in all the heathen nations, the sun was adored. Sunday was evidently a rival to God's ancient Sabbath, as idolatry was a grand counterfeit system to the worship of the true God. In proof of these statements we cite various authorities, all of them persons who did not observe the seventh day, but the first day of the week, as far as they observed any day. Webster thus defines the word Sunday :—

"Sunday; so called because this day was anciently dedicated to the sun, or to its worship. The first day of the week."

Worcester, also, in his large dictionary thus defines it :—

"Sunday; so named because anciently dedicated to the sun or to its worship. The first day of the week."

The *North British Review*, in a labored attempt to justify the observance of Sunday by the Christian world, styles the day,—

"THE WILD SOLAR HOLIDAY [*i. e.*, festival in honor of the sun] OF ALL PAGAN TIMES."—Vol. 18, p. 409.

This, from such an intelligent authority, is certainly a strong proof of the general regard for the Sunday among the heathen. It is indeed surprising how Sunday should thus generally have come to be a holiday *each week*. This is strong evidence of the antiquity of the weekly division of time.

Verstegan says :—

"The most ancient Germans being pagans, and having appropriated their first day of the week to the peculiar adoration of the sun, whereof that day doth yet in our English tongue retain the name of Sunday."—*Verstegan's Antiquities*, p. 10. London, 1628.

Again he says:—

"Unto the day dedicated unto the special adoration of the idol of the sun, they gave the name of Sunday, as much as to say, the sun's day, or the day of the sun. This idol was placed in a temple, and there adored and sacrificed unto, for that they believed that the sun in the firmament did with or in this idol correspond and co-operate."—*Idem*, p. 68.

Jennings, speaking of the time of the deliverance of the Israelites from Egyptian bondage, thus speaks of the Gentile nations as—

"The idolatrous nations who, in honor to their chief god, the sun, began their day at his rising."—*Jewish Antiquities*, book 3, chap. 1.

Again:—

"The day which the heathens in general consecrated to the worship and honor of their chief god, the sun, which, according to our computation, was the first day of the week."—*Idem*, chap. 3.

We see, therefore, according to this author, that Sunday was more ancient than the coming of Israel out of Egypt.

Morer says:—

"It is not to be denied but we borrow the name of this day from the ancient Greeks and Romans, and we allow that the old Egyptians worshiped the sun, and as a standing *memorial* of their veneration, dedicated this day to him. And we find by the influence of their examples, *other* nations, and among them the Jews themselves, doing him homage."—*Dialogues on the Lord's Day*, pp. 22, 23.

These statements of respectable authors place Sunday in the very earliest ages of antiquity, as a "*memorial*" of the first form of idolatry among the Egyptians, from whom the Romans and the Greeks largely derived their forms of heathen worship. It is well known that their most famous philosophers went to Egypt to become acquainted with their *sacred mysteries*. Among the Assyrians and Persians, two other very ancient nations, it is well known that Sabianism—the worship of the sun, moon, and stars—was the most ancient form of religion. Thus sun-worship, with its attendant "*memorial*," was struggling for recognition away back in the earliest ages, and that, too, in direct antagonism with the "*memorial*" of Jehovah's rest, the Sabbath of the Lord.

No one can fully grasp the Sabbath and Sunday question without viewing it in these extended relations. The change of the Sabbath is the result of one of the deepest plans ever conceived by the author of all evil. As the Sabbath is the memorial of God's creative power, a grand monument of the work which shows his divinity as an omnipotent being, Satan aims against it his most cunning schemes, to set it aside and to put in its place a day which commemorates false worship and apostasy from God. We have seen that the Sunday holiday was regarded throughout the whole heathen world, even in the earliest ages before the exodus from Egypt.

Though not exactly in the line of the argument we are now considering, we cannot refrain from noticing the position of the Sabbath among the Gentile nations in this first **great struggle** with its rival, the Sunday.

This reference will be valuable, inasmuch as it proves the existence of the Sabbath among other nations, long before it was specially committed to the Jewish people for preservation till the knowledge of the true God should be once more restored to those nations who had wandered into idolatry.

Calmet gives the following :—

> "Manasseh Ben Israel assures us that, according to the tradition of the ancients, Abraham and his posterity, having preserved the memory of creation, observed the Sabbath also, in consequence of natural law to that purpose. It is also believed that the religion of the seventh day is preserved among the pagans; and the observance of this day is as old as the world itself. Almost all the philosophers and poets acknowledge the seventh day holy."

This statement that Abraham observed the Sabbath is in perfect harmony with the statement in the book of Genesis, that Abraham "kept my charge, my commandments, my statutes, and my laws," and with the fact that in that age they reckoned time by weeks. Gen. 26:5; 29:27. We know that the Sabbath was in existence before the law was given on Sinai, because the children of Israel kept it a month before the promulgation of that law; and God set it apart at the creation. Gen. 2:1-3; Ex. 16. Abraham, who came from the Assyrian country, kept the Sabbath; and this writer intimates that it was known among all the ancient nations.

The Arabs are also a very ancient nation. They existed in Abraham's time. William Jones, missionary to Palestine, says :—

> "The seventh day is known throughout Arabdom by 'Yom-es-Sabt,' or day of the Sabbath. Neither the word

'seven' nor any other name is given by the Arabs to the Sabbath day. It is always the Sabbath; and the reason for it, they say, is that this has been its name from the beginning."

This is valuable testimony. The Arabs were never united with the Jews. They have always inhabited the country in which they settled in Abraham's time, and have nearly always maintained an independent existence as a people.

Gilfillan says:—

"It would appear that the Chinese, who have now no Sabbath, at one time honored the seventh day of the week."—*The Sabbath*, p. 360.

The *Asiatic Journal* has this item:—

"The prime minister of the empire affirms that the Sabbath was anciently observed by the Chinese, in conformity to the directions of the king."

On page 359 he says:—

"The Phœnicians, according to Porphyry, 'consecrated the seventh day as holy.'"

Josephus bears this testimony:—

"There is not any city of the Grecians, nor any of the barbarians, nor any nation whatsoever, whither our custom of resting on the seventh day has not come."—*Against Apion*, book 2, par. 40.

Gilfillan says:—

"The Greeks and Romans, according to Aretius, consecrated Saturday to rest, conceiving it unfit for civil actions and warlike affairs, but suited for contemplation."—*The Sabbath*, p. 363.

John G. Butler, a Free-will Baptist author, says:—

"We learn also from the testimony of Philo, Hesiod, Josephus, Porphyry, and others, that the division of time into weeks and the observance of the seventh day were common to the nations of antiquity. They would not have adopted such a custom from the Jews. Whence, then, could it have been derived, but through tradition, from its original institution in the Garden of Eden?"—*Natural and Revealed Theology*, p. 396.

Archbishop Usher gives the following:—

"The very Gentiles, both civil and barbarous, both ancient and of later days, as it were by *universal* kind of tradition, retained the distinction of the seventh day of the week."—*Usher's Works*, part 1, chap. 4.

Hesiod (B. C. 870) says:—

"The seventh day is sacred."

Homer (B. C. 907) says:—

"Then cometh the seventh day, that is sacred."

Tibulus says:—

"Bad omens detained me on the sacred day of Saturn."

We come now to one of the most interesting discoveries of modern times. In the investigations of the ancient ruins of Nineveh and Babylon during the past fifty years, many marvelous things have been brought to the light of day,—things showing an extensive knowledge of the arts and sciences, which have been lost for ages, and among them are ancient monuments and tablets, on which historical facts were sculptured. Learned men have, after much investigation, been enabled to read these inscriptions, and many facts have been obtained which corroborate the record of the Holy Scriptures. Among others, records have been discovered showing conclusively that in those early times the seventh-day Sabbath was observed. We quote from the *Congregationalist* (Boston), Nov. 15, 1882 :—

"Mr. George Smith says in his 'Assyrian Discoveries' (1875) : 'In the year 1869, I discovered, among other things, a curious religious calendar of the Assyrians, in which every month is divided into four weeks, and the seventh days, or Sabbaths, are marked out as days on which no work should be undertaken.' Again, in his 'History of Assur-bani-pal,' he says, 'The 7th, 14th, 19th, 21st, and 28th [days of the month] are described by an ideogram equivalent to *sulu* or *sulum*, meaning "rest." The calendar contains lists of work forbidden to be done on these days, which evidently correspond to the Sabbaths of the Jews."

H. Fox Talbot, F. R. S., one of the learned Assyriologists of Europe, says of the fifth "Creation Tablet" found by Mr. George Smith on the opposite side of ancient Nineveh, on the bank of the Tigris, and now to be seen in the British Museum :—

"This fifth tablet is very important, because it affirms clearly, in my opinion, that the origin of the Sabbath was coeval with the creation. . . . It has been known for some time, that the Babylonians observed the Sabbath with considerable strictness. On that day the king was not allowed to take a drive in his chariot ; various meats were forbidden to be eaten ; and there were a number of other minute restrictions. . . . But it is not known that they believed the Sabbath to have been ordained at creation. I have found, however, since the translation of the fifth tablet was completed, that Mr. Sayce has recently published a similar opinion. See the *Academy* of Nov. 27, 1875, p. 554."—*Records of the Past*, vol. 4, pp. 117, 118.

A. H. Sayce, in his lecture before the Royal Institution concerning the Assyrian tablets discovered in the excavations on the site of ancient Babylon, says:—

"The Sabbath of the seventh day appears to have been observed with great strictness; even the monarch was forbidden to eat cooked meat, change his clothes, take medicine, or drive his chariot on that day."—*Northern Christian Advocate.*

Here we have testimony, which could be greatly multiplied, showing that away back in the earliest ages the Chinese, Phœnicians, Assyrians, Babylonians, Arabians, Greeks, and Romans, and many other nations, did regard the Sabbath as a sacred day. The farther we get back, the more sacredly they seemed to regard it. It is not surprising that Abraham, who came from Assyria, was a Sabbath-keeper. These tablets were engraved long before histories, in the ordinary sense of the term, were written; or at least none so ancient are extant, unless it be the books of Moses. Yet these facts were preserved all these ages on the tablets of stone, and now come to light as testimony to the sacredness of the Sabbath from the most ancient nations.

But let the thoughtful reader notice the striking fact that when idolatry came to prevail fully, and sun-worship became general among all the nations but the Jews, the Sabbath gradually disappeared, and the Sunday, the "*memorial*" of idolatry, took its place in general esteem. It is in the earliest record of these nations that we find references to the Sabbath. In the later ones there are very few. Satan, the author of false worship, suppressed the Sabbath wherever his influence was paramount.

But God chose the children of Abraham because this devout man kept his charge, his commandments, his statutes, and his laws. He surrounded them with special circumstances, customs, and ordinances, to keep them from the heathen nations around them, till the "seed"—Christ—should come, through whom all the nations of the world should be blessed, by the calling of the Gentiles again. God gave himself to that people, and with himself *his great "memorial," the Sabbath*, which kept in mind his work at creation. The other nations once had it; but through their idolatry, God and his memorial were nearly forgotten by them. Satan tried his best to rob God's chosen people of this keepsake; but because of God's chastisements and the constant warnings of the prophets, he could not quite accomplish this work.

After Christ came, and the apostles were sent to the Gentiles, they carried with them, as we have shown, the Sabbath of the Lord. The early Christians kept it as Christ and the apostles had done; and as Christianity spread abroad to all the nations of the earth, the two "memorials" once more came in conflict. The Sunday "*holiday of all pagan times*" was intrenched among all the nations. The people everywhere regarded it as a special day of pleasure and recreation. It came every week. This fact made it difficult for those who kept the seventh day as the Sabbath, something in the same manner as it makes it difficult now for those who turn from the observance of Sunday to the Sabbath. All who have tried it, know well how hard it is.

Gradually, after a generation or two, the sense of sacredness began to weaken, and feelings of expediency were cherished. The great struggle between the two memorials then began, and continued, as we shall see, till the Sabbath of the Lord was generally abandoned.

These influences are well presented by a clergyman of the Church of England, Mr. Chafie, who published in 1652 a work in vindication of first-day observance. After showing the general observance of Sunday by the heathen world in the early ages of the church, he thus states the reasons which forbid Christians' attempting to keep any other day :—

"1. Because of the contempt, scorn, and derision they thereby should be had in, among all the Gentiles with whom they lived. . . . How grievous would be their taunts and reproaches against the poor Christians living with them and under their power for their new-set sacred day, had the Christians chosen any other than the Sunday. . . . 2. Most Christians then were either servants or of the poorer sort of people ; and the Gentiles, most probably, would not give their servants liberty to cease from working on any other set day constantly, except on their Sunday. . . 3. Because, had they assayed such a change, it would have been but labor in vain ; . . . they could never have brought it to pass."—*The Seventh-day Sabbath*, pp. 61, 62.

These reasons present powerful inducements which we cannot deny to those who regard expediency more than principle. The early church had begun already to apostatize from God, and to accept traditions in preference to the Scriptures. Many of the early Fathers had been heathen philosophers. It ever comes natural for human nature, when it changes its religious belief, to take with it more or less of the old notions and practices.

Gradually the church began to be less strict in its observance of Bible truths, and to conform more and more to the spirit of the world around them. No Protestant will dispute this in reference to their regard to many of the gospel requirements. Many thought by uniting more or less with their heathen neighbors they would be more likely to convert them. In this way the Sabbath partially lost its sacredness, and the first day gained in position and influence.

Morer, after stating the fact that the first day of the week, as we have quoted, had long been the "memorial" of sun-worship, as its name, "Sunday," implies, places before us the reasons why the church was led to adopt it :—

"These abuses did not hinder the Fathers of the Christian Church simply to repeal, or altogether lay by, the day or its name, but only to sanctify and improve both, as they did also the pagan temples polluted before with idolatrous services, and other instances wherein those good men were always tender to work any other change than what was evidently necessary, and in such things as were plainly inconsistent with the Christian religion ; so that Sunday being the day on which the Gentiles solemnly adored that planet, and called it Sunday, . . . the Christians thought fit to keep the same day and the same name of it, that they might not appear causelessly peevish, and by that means hinder the conversion of the Gentiles, and bring a greater prejudice than might be otherwise taken against the gospel."— *Dialogues on the Lord's Day*, pp. 22, 23.

It is such politic reasoning as this which has always led to apostasy and conformity to the world. It finally developed fully into the Roman Catholic Church, a mixture of heathenism and Christianity. This conformity to the heathen custom of regarding Sunday as a festival day, was carried so far that many thought the Christians worshiped the sun as a god; so that Tertullian, one of the Christian Fathers, defended them from this charge. He answered that though they worshiped toward the east, like the heathen, they did it for another reason than sun-worship. He acknowledged that these acts—prayer toward the east, and making Sunday a day of festivity—did give men a chance to think the sun was the god of the Christians. (See *Apology*, chap. 67, sec. 16.)

Tertullian is therefore a witness to the fact that Sunday was a heathen festival when it was adopted by the Christian church, and that they were taunted with being sun-worshipers.

When we see the striking changes which have occurred in the manner of observing Sunday within the past one or two hundred years, even when nearly all regard it with more or less sacredness, and when we note the general laxity of practice as compared with the strictness of our ancestors, we cannot wonder at the changes which two or three centuries produced when strong influences were brought to bear against the Sabbath, and so many other perversions of Bible doctrines were introduced. Thus we see how these two causes—the general regard for Sunday as a weekly heathen holiday, and the difficulty of keeping the seventh day where Sunday observance was almost universal—

would powerfully tend to discourage those who kept the Sabbath, and gradually undermine it in the esteem of all.

CHAPTER XIII.

OTHER REASONS WHY SUNDAY WAS FAVORED.

THE general observance of memorial days in the second and third centuries of the Christian era, was also another reason why Sunday was exalted. Doubtless the practice was innocent at first, and originated from the best motives, being prompted by reverence for Christ. The same principle in the human heart which has always led people to commemorate important events in which they have felt a deep interest, by celebrating with appropriate services the special days upon which these events occurred, led the disciples, after the apostles' death, to regard with more or less interest the days of Christ's betrayal, crucifixion, resurrection, and ascension. To this day, Good Friday, Holy Thursday, etc., are considered as quite sacred in the state churches of Europe, especially in the Roman and Greek Catholic churches. "Holy week," as the week connected with the last scenes in Christ's life is called, has been regarded with great reverence for ages in the Catholic and other national churches, and is really becoming popular in many Protestant churches. But all such services and observances have no authority in Scripture; they are derived from tradition alone. It was in this way that Sunday, the day of Christ's resurrection, first became prominent among Christians. At first it was little, if any, more prominent than Friday, the day of his crucifixion. Mosheim says:—

"It is also probable that Friday, the day of Christ's crucifixion, was early distinguished by particular honors from the other days of the week."—*Eccl. Hist.*, cent. 1, part 2, chap. 4, note ‡ to sec. 4.

He says of the second century:—

"Many also observed the fourth day of the week, on which Christ was betrayed; and the sixth, which was the day of his crucifixion."—*Idem*, cent. 2, part 2, chap. 1, sec. 12.

Dr. Peter Heylyn says of those who chose Sunday:—

"Because our Saviour rose that day from among the dead, so chose they Friday for another, by reason of our Saviour's passion, and Wednesday, on the which he had been betrayed; the Saturday, or ancient Sabbath, being meanwhile retained in the Eastern churches."—*History of the Sabbath*, part 2, chap. 1, sec. 12.

Of the comparative sacredness of these voluntary festivals, the same writer testifies:—

"If we consider either the preaching of the word, the ministration of the sacraments, or the public prayers, the Sunday in the Eastern churches had no great prerogative above other days, especially above the Wednesday and the Friday, save that the meetings were more solemn, and the concourse of people greater than at other times, as is most likely."—*Idem*, part 2, chap. 3, sec. 4.

But the fact that Sunday was a general public holiday of the heathen world around them, and that the Church of Rome made persistent efforts to give it precedence, and, above all, the effect of Constantine's decree in its favor, gave the Sunday at last a great superiority over these other voluntary festival days, as well as over the Sabbath itself. The efforts of the Church of Rome, and those in sympathy with it, in behalf of Sunday, making it a day of joy and gladness, freedom from fasts, etc., at the same time turning the Sabbath into a fast day, as we have seen, did much toward giving prestige and dignity to the former.

The first recorded instance of Sunday observance which has any claim to be considered genuine, is mentioned by Justin Martyr, A. D. 140, in an address to the Roman emperor. He states in substance that the Christians met together on Sunday, when the writings of the apostles and prophets were read, a discourse was given, prayers offered, the consecrated elements—bread and wine and water—distributed to, and partaken of by, all that were present, and sent to the absent by the hands of the deacons, and a collection taken up, etc. We here see some innovations introduced, such as sending the emblems to the absent, and using water in connection with them. He does not intimate that this day had any divine authority from Christ and the apostles, or any command whatever for its observance. It would seem to be a purely voluntary practice. Neither does he hint that the day was regarded as a Sabbath, or that it was wrong to work on that day. He only states that they held a religious meeting on it. Sunday had not, up to this time, acquired any title of sacredness. It bore simply its old heathen title. He does not call it the Lord's day, nor the Christian Sabbath. It is more than fifty years later before a recorded instance can be found where it was called by the former, and many years elapsed before it was called by the latter title.

Perhaps it will be proper at this point to introduce the testimony of Neander, the greatest of church historians. This German author speaks as follows of Sunday observance in the early church:—

"The festival of Sunday, like all other festivals, was always only a human ordinance, and it was far from the intentions of the apostles to establish a divine command in this respect,—far from them, and from the early apostolic church, to transfer the laws of the Sabbath to Sunday. Perhaps at the end of the second century a false application of this kind had begun to take place; for men appear by that time to have considered laboring on Sunday as a sin."—*Neander's Church History*, translated by Rose, p. 186.

This statement of this eminent authority truly gives the origin of Sunday observance; it was purely voluntary, standing solely upon human authority. Sir Wm. Domville states the same fact:—

"Not any ecclesiastical writer of the first three centuries attributed the origin of Sunday observance either to Christ or to his apostles."—*Examination of the Six Texts*, Supplement, pp. 6, 7.

The authors living nearest the days of the apostles never heard of the arguments put forth at this remote day for the change of the Sabbath. For hundreds of years no hints, even, were given that Christ or the apostles changed the Sabbath. We have seen before that Victor, bishop of Rome, A. D. 196, made an edict in behalf of Sunday, trying to compel the other churches to celebrate the passover on that day. Also that the same church turned the Sabbath into a fast-day, to place a stigma upon it.

We will next notice the efforts of the Roman Church and its sympathizers to make Sunday a very joyful festival, in opposition to the Sabbath, which it had thus stigmatized as a day of sorrow and fasting. It was considered a sin to fast on Sunday ; and on that day they must stand, not kneel, during prayer, this act of standing in prayer being a symbol of the resurrection. Tertullian, the oldest of the Latin Fathers, who wrote about A. D. 200, says :—

"We devote Sunday to rejoicing."—*Apologeticus*, par. 16.

Dr. Heylyn says :—

"Tertullian tells us that they did devote Sunday partly unto mirth and recreation, not to devotion altogether ; when in a hundred years after Tertullian's time there was no law or constitution to restrain men from labor on this day in the Christian church."—*History of the Sabbath*, part 2, chap. 8, sec. 13.

Tertullian himself says :—

"We count fasting or kneeling in worship on the Lord's day to be unlawful. We rejoice in the same privilege also from Easter to Whitsunday."—*De Corona*, sec. 3.

From Peter of Alexandria, another Father, we quote the following :—

"But the Lord's day we celebrate as a day of joy, because on it he rose again, on which day we have received it for a custom not even to bow the knee."— *Canon 15.*

We could give many other similar statements, but it is not necessary. We will not, however, omit one statement from Tertullian. In speaking of "offerings for the dead," the manner of Sunday observance, and the use of the sign of the cross upon the forehead, he gives the ground of these observances as follows :—

"If for these and other such rules you insist upon having positive Scripture injunction, you will find none. Tradition will be held forth to you as the originator of them, custom as their strengthener, and faith as their observer."—*De Corona,* sec. 4.

Truly, this is a frank statement, which cannot be disputed. In this statement we have presented, clearly and boldly, one of the reasons why Sunday gradually advanced in sacredness in the popular view, the acceptance of tradition instead of the word of God being the real ground of first-day observance, as well as of a vast number of other doctrines and customs which came into the church at this time. Tradition *vs.* Scripture is the great point of difference between Catholicism and Protestantism. The moment we admit tradition as proper authority for religious duty, we step down from the Protestant rock, and can find no good reason why we should not receive all the heterogeneous practices of the Catholic Church.

We close this part of the subject, relating to the authority for Sunday-keeping previous to the edict of Constantine, by giving the conclusions of one who has spent many years in investigating the writings of the early Fathers. He gives the substance of their testimony concerning the earliest observance of Sunday as follows :—

"We shall find, 1. That no one claimed for first-day observance any divine authority ; 2. That none of them had ever heard of the change of the Sabbath, and none believed the first-day festival to be a continuation of the Sabbatic institution ; 3. That labor on that day is never set forth as sinful, and that abstinence from labor is never mentioned as a feature of its observance, nor even implied, only so far as is necessary in order to spend a portion of the day in worship ; 4. That if we put together all the hints respecting Sunday observance which are scattered through the Fathers of the first three centuries (for no one of them gives more than two of these, and generally a single hint is all that is found in one writer), we shall find just four items : (1.) An assembly on that day in which the Bible was read and expounded, and the supper celebrated, and money collected ; (2.) The day must be one of rejoicing ; (3.) It must not be a day of fasting ; and (4.) The knee must not be bent in prayer on that day."—*Andrews's History of the Sabbath*, pp. 285, 286.

CHAPTER XIV.

A LAW FOR RESTING ON SUNDAY.

WE have now reached an important point in the consideration of the advance of the Sunday institution. We have seen it creeping stealthily into prominence, in various ways, through one influence or another, until it has become quite generally recognized as a day for religious meetings. But hitherto it has never claimed Sabbatic honors. Not a single instance can be found of any law given in its favor as a day of rest, and no instance of its being observed as a Sabbath, of its taking that title, or being recognized in that character.

For three hundred years of church history the rulers of the Roman empire had been pagans. In the early part of the fourth century there came a change ; Constantine the Great, so called, professed the Christian religion. Before this, because of persecution, the church had maintained some degree of purity, though many practices had been adopted for which there was no warrant in Scripture. But from this time on, most rapid changes were seen. To obtain favor with the emperor, with their own profit in view, vast multitudes of pagans embraced the Christian religion nominally, though at heart they remained unchanged. All Protestants admit that the age of Constantine and the one immediately succeeding were periods of great corruption. From this time forward the process was most rapid, till it finally culminated in the full development of the Roman Catholic Church. We shall see that during this very time the most rapid advance of the Sunday institution also occurs.

In the year A. D. 321, Constantine issued the following edict :—

"Let all the judges and town people, and the occupation of all trades, rest on the venerable day of the sun; but let those who are situated in the country, freely and at full liberty attend to the business of agriculture ; because it often happens that no other day is so fit for sowing corn and planting vines; lest, the critical moment being let slip, men should lose the commodities granted by Heaven."

In no document, human or divine, can any command be found to rest on Sunday, the first day of the week, previous to this law by Constantine. Let the discerning reader note carefully the language of this famous law. It does not command us to rest on the Christian Sabbath, on the first day of the week, or the Lord's day, or on the day in which Christians generally meet to have divine worship; but it is the "*venerable day of the sun*" which is thus honored,—"*the wild solar holiday of all pagan times.*" The reader will recall what has been stated in former chapters concerning the conflict between the two "memorials," the one of the Creator's rest, the other of the earliest form of idolatry—sun-worship. Constantine, with the arm of civil law, now strikes the first heavy blow in behalf of the "venerable day of the sun," thus strengthening the positions taken concerning the antiquity of the heathen custom of sun-worship on the first day of the week. It was, then, a very "*venerable*" day in the year 321. Constantine was still a heathen when he put forth this decree. This edict went into effect on the seventh day of March. The day following, viz., March 8, 321, another heathen decree was issued, the purport of which was,—

"That if any royal edifice should be struck by lightning, the ancient ceremonies of propitiating the deity should be practiced, and the haruspices were to be consulted to learn the meaning of the awful portent. The haruspices were soothsayers who foretold future events by examining the entrails of beasts slaughtered in sacrifice to the gods."— *Andrews's History of the Sabbath*, pp. 347, 348, ed. 1887.

Any one who has read heathen history knows this was a practice very common among them.

Constantine was a worshiper of Apollo, or the sun. Thus Gibbon says:—

"The devotion of Constantine was more peculiarly directed to the genius of the sun, the Apollo of Greek and Roman mythology; and he was pleased to be represented with the symbols of the god of light and poetry. . . . The altars of Apollo were crowned with the votive offerings of Constantine; and the credulous multitude were taught to believe that the emperor was permitted to behold with mortal eyes the visible majesty of their tutelar deity. . . . The sun was universally celebrated as the invincible guide and protector of Constantine."— *Decline and Fall of the Roman Empire*, chap. 20, par. 3.

Here we plainly discern the reason why the emperor puts forth this decree in favor of the "venerable day of the sun." He was an ardent worshiper of the sun. Mosheim places the nominal conversion of Constantine two years later than the edict. We say "nominal" conversion, for there is no good reason to believe that he was ever a genuine Christian. He was a tyrant, a murderer of many innocent persons, and gave evidence of being anything but a follower of the Prince of peace.

The first law for keeping Sunday as a day of rest, then, was a heathen law in favor of sun-worship. This is admitted by many of the best Protestant historians and authors. Dr. Milman, the learned editor of Gibbon, says:—

"The rescript commanding the celebration of the Christian Sabbath bears no allusion to its peculiar sanctity as a Christian institution. It is the day of the sun, which is to be observed by the general veneration. The courts were to be closed, and the noise and tumult of public business and legal litigation were no longer to violate the repose of the sacred day. But the believer in the new paganism, of which the solar worship was the characteristic, might acquiesce without scruple in the sanctity of the first day of the week." — *History of Christianity*, book 3, chap. 1, p. 396, ed. 1881.

In a subsequent chapter he adds: —

"In fact, as we have before observed, the day of the sun would be willingly hallowed by almost all the pagan world, especially that part which had admitted any tendency toward the Oriental theology." — *Idem*, book 3, chap. 4, p. 397.

Thus it is fully admitted that the design of this decree was wholly pagan. It was a step in the great contest which had been going on for ages to crowd out the Sabbath of the Lord, and exalt the "memorial" of idolatry in its place. How did this heathen edict affect the practice of the Christian church? We have already seen that the two days, the seventh and the first, were balancing in popular favor, and that the Roman Church had been doing what it could to suppress the Sabbath and exalt Sunday. We shall now see that the so-called Church of Jesus Christ took advantage of this heathen decree in behalf of the "venerable day of the sun," to complete the work already begun. This edict was a heavy blow to the Sabbath, and as great an aid to the Sunday. We quote from the "Encyclopedia Britannica" as follows:—

"It was Constantine the Great who first made a law for the proper observance of Sunday, and who, according to Eusebius, appointed it should be regularly celebrated throughout the Roman empire. Before him, and even in his time, they observed the Jewish Sabbath, as well as Sunday. . . . By Constantine's law, promulgated in 321, it was decreed that for the future the Sunday should be kept as a day of rest in all cities and towns; but he allowed the country people to follow their work."—Art. Sunday, seventh edition, 1842.

Mosheim, who was quite a strong advocate for Sunday, says of this law:—

"The first day of the week, which was the ordinary and stated time for the public assemblies of the Christians, was, in consequence of a peculiar law enacted by Constantine, observed with greater solemnity than it had formerly been."—*Ecclesiastical History*, cent. 4, part 2, chap. 4, sec. 5.

This is quite an admission for this historian to make. This heathen law, permitting those who followed the occupation of agriculture to plow, sow, plant trees, etc., but which forbade the town people to work, caused the Christians to observe Sunday more strictly than they had formerly. As the law only required a part of the people to rest on Sunday, while the others could freely work, we must conclude that before the issue of this edict, *none* of the people had refrained from labor on Sunday. This we have seen was the case, since there was no law in existence before this requiring it. Sir Wm. Domville says:—

"Centuries of the Christian era passed away before the Sunday was observed by the Christian church as a Sabbath. History does not furnish us with a single proof or indication that it was at any time so observed previous to the Sabbatical edict of Constantine in A. D. 321."—*Examination of the Six Texts*, p. 291.

This edict of Constantine's greatly accelerated the current already setting strongly against the ancient Sabbath. It furnished *some* authority, if it was only heathen, in behalf of the Sunday. Every advance it made correspondingly depressed the Sabbath, inasmuch as keeping two days in each week as a rest day would be absurd. An able writer thus expresses the result throughout the Roman empire :—

"Very shortly after the period when Constantine issued his edict enjoining the general observance of Sunday throughout the Roman empire, the party that had contended for the observance of the seventh day dwindled into insignificance. The observance of Sunday as a public festival, during which all business, with the exception of rural employments, was intermitted, came to be more and more generally established ever after this time, throughout both the Greek and the Latin churches. There is no evidence, however, that either at this or at a period much later the observance was viewed as deriving any obligation from the fourth commandment ; it seems to have been regarded as an institution corresponding in nature with Christmas, Good Friday, and other festivals of the church ; and as resting with them on the ground of ecclesiastical authority and tradition."—*Cox's Sabbath Laws*, pp. 280, 281.

We see, therefore, that that which caused the Sabbath to be greatly neglected was the heathen decree of the emperor. Heathenism and corrupted Christianity united their forces in putting down the Sabbath and exalting Sunday in its place. It might be said that this decree was the expiring act of heathenism. In one sense it was so ; but the kind of Christianity which took its place really resembled heathenism more than it did the pure and humble religion of Christ and his apostles. This remark at first may seem harsh and incredible ; but truly the reflecting, observing mind must admit its truthfulness. What resemblance is there between the plain, simple forms of worship observable in the ministry of Christ and the apostles, and the gorgeous, pompous ceremonials of the Catholic Church? What resemblance is there in the appearance, manners, and dress of the two,—in our Saviour going about on foot, a man of sorrows and acquainted with grief, healing the sick and benefiting all, clad in his seamless coat, the garb of the poor, and the lordly priest, clad in his official robes of purple or scarlet, bowing before images with his train of attendants, and exacting the highest homage? What resemblance is there in the doctrines of the two? Christ taught the need of repentance, faith, baptism, and the living of a humble, pure, holy life of obedience to the truths of God's word and the principles of God's law. But look at the Catholic ceremonials, the confessions to the priest, the prayers for souls in purgatory, the holy water, vows of celibacy, worshiping of images, elevating and adoring the bread, believing it to be the actual flesh of our Lord and Saviour!

And what resemblance is there in the *spirit* of the two? Our Saviour was ever seeking to alleviate suffering, to benefit all within his reach. He wept over the people of Jerusalem because they would not let him save them; he prayed, even for his enemies, while hanging on the cross in the greatest agony. On the other hand, look at the bloody Crusades, at the massacre on St. Bartholomew's day, when the blood of the poor Huguenots ran down the streets of Paris, when the papists surprised them through deception ; and look at the poor Waldenses, butchered by thousands—men, women, and children—because they would not take the pope's authority instead of the Scriptures as their rule of action. See the Inquisition with its horrors ; men and women tortured on the rack, or starved to death in deep dungeons. These things were done when the Roman Church had the power. What, we say, are the resemblances between their practices and the pure religion of Jesus?

But there is a striking resemblance on the other hand between heathenism and the ceremonies, manners, forms of worship, bowing to images, resplendent robes, and persecuting spirit of Catholicism ; indeed, Catholics themselves admit that many of their customs were derived from the heathen. On this interesting point we will venture to quote from two eminent Catholic writers. Cardinal Baronius, perhaps the most reliable writer in this church, says : —

"That many things have been laudibly translated from Gentile superstition into the Christian religion, hath been demonstrated by many examples and the authority of the Fathers. And what wonder if the most holy bishops have granted that the most ancient customs of the Gentiles should be introduced into the worship of the true God, from which it seemed impossible to take off many, though converted to Christianity ?"

Bervaldus, another Catholic writer, speaks as follows :—

"When I call to mind the institutions of the holy mysteries of the heathen, I am forced to believe that most things appertaining to the celebration of our solemnities and ceremonies are taken thence ; as, for example, from the Gentile religion the shaven heads of priests, turning round of the altar, sacrificial pomps, and many such like ceremonies which our priests solemnly use in our mysteries. *How many things in our religion are like the Roman religion! How many rites common!"*

Truly our remark that Catholicism resembles the heathen worship more than it does the religion of Christ, cannot be denied. Catholicism is a system of mixed Christianity and heathenism, with the latter predominating.

The edict by Constantine, and the full adoption of the heathen Sunday by the church, marks the point where this heathen union was consummated. Constantine at that point represented the heathen, being an ardent sun-worshiper. Pope Sylvester, at that time bishop of Rome, represented the Catholic Church. In its efforts to elevate Sunday, this church joyfully accepted his heathen decree and heathen day, and thus fully blended the heathen system with their corrupted form of Christianity. From that point the barriers were broken down, and heathens and heathenism largely took possession of the church. At this point, so history informs us, many of the humble, God-fearing Christians withdrew into retired places, where they could still worship God according to the Scriptures. Pope Sylvester, by his apostolical authority, changed the name of the day, giving it the imposing title of "Lord's Day." (See "Ecclesiastical History of Lucius," cent. 4, cap. 10, pp. 739, 740.) It had been called by that title by a few writers before ; but

Sylvester, as head of the church, now officially decided that its title should be "Lord's Day." Thus Constantine elevated the Sunday as a heathen festival to be observed throughout the empire, while Sylvester changed it into a Christian institution, dignifying it by the title of "Lord's Day."

Concerning the grounds upon which Sunday stands, we will here give a quotation from Dr. Heylyn :—

"Thus do we see upon what grounds the Lord's day stands: *on custom first* and *voluntary* consecration of it to religious meetings; that custom countenanced by the authority of the church of God, which *tacitly* approved the same; and *finally confirmed and ratified by Christian princes* throughout their empires. And as the day for rest from labors and restraint from business upon that day, [it] received its greatest strength from the supreme magistrate as long as he retained that power which to him belongs; as after from the canons and decrees of councils, the decretals of popes and orders of particular prelates, when the sole managing of ecclesiastical affairs was committed to them."—*History of the Sabbath*, part 2, chap. 3, sec. 12.

Here we have truly set before us the authority on which the Sunday Sabbath rests. How different from that for the Sabbath of the Lord! The former is wholly human; the latter, wholly divine. The former originated in heathenism and idolatry, and was finally adopted as a rest day by a corrupted church on the authority of a Roman tyrant; the latter began by the act of God himself, at the creation of the world, in resting, blessing, and setting apart the day for man to keep, and in commanding his people to observe it for all time.

Eusebius, who was a bishop, and a great flatterer and favorite of the Emperor Constantine, seems to admit that the change wrought in the Sabbath at this time was by human authority. He says:—

"All things whatsoever that it was duty to do on the Sabbath, these we have transferred to the Lord's day." — *Cox's Sabbath Literature*, vol. 1, p. 361.

We see at last a change of the Sabbath quite fully wrought; at least to this extent, that the Sabbath was degraded by a Catholic council, and denounced under a curse as heretical, and that the Sunday was generally considered a day for public worship, and for at least partial rest. We will next notice other steps by which the latter was rendered still more sacred in the eyes of the people.

CHAPTER XV.

SUNDAY DOWN TO THE REFORMATION.

HAVING noticed quite carefully the steps by which Sunday reached an influential position in the time of Constantine, it will not be necessary to cite many more authorities. We will only give a few evidences showing how the Romish Church still carefully fostered this favorite child, and left nothing undone that it could do to render it more sacred. It will be remembered that the important decree by Constantine, which was the first command in behalf of Sunday requiring any one to rest on the first day of the week, gave permission to those engaged in agriculture to work on that day. It was not long until this permission was set aside, and all were commanded to rest on the venerable Sunday.

Pope Leo took certain steps in the fifth century to make up the deficiencies in the Sunday laws, and add to the honor of this favorite institution. He required that all ordinations should be conferred on this day and no other. Heylyn says :—

"A law [was] made by Leo, then pope of Rome, and generally since taken up in the Western church, that they should be conferred upon no day else."—*History of the Sabbath*, part 2, chap. 4, sec. 8.

According to Dr. Justin Edwards, this same pope made this decree in behalf of Sunday :—

"*We ordain*, according to the true meaning of the Holy Ghost, and of the apostles as thereby directed, that on the sacred day wherein our own integrity was restored, all do rest and cease from labor."—*Sabbath Manual*, p. 123.

Emperor Leo, A. D. 469, put forth the following decree in behalf of Sunday :—

"It is our will and pleasure, that the holy days dedicated to the most high God, should not be spent in sensual recreations, or otherwise profaned by suits of law, especially the Lord's day, which we decree to be a venerable day, and therefore free it of all citations, executions, pleadings, and the like avocations. . . . If any will presume to offend in the premises, if he be a military man, let him lose his commission ; or if other, let his estate or goods be confiscated. . . . We command, therefore, all, as well husbandmen as others, to forbear work on this day of our restoration."—*Dialogues on the Lord's Day*, pp. 259, 260.

Here we see, first, the pope ordaining that all cease from labor on Sunday. Then the emperor steps in and supports this action. Full human authority is now given to rest on Sunday. All classes must obey, on penalty of fines or confiscation of all their property. We do not wonder, then, that in that age, when few had Bibles, and tradition was generally followed, Sunday came to be generally observed. We learn that just previous to this time, however, Sunday was not very strictly observed as a rest day.

Kitto says :—

"Chrysostom (A. D. 360) concludes one of his homilies by dismissing his audience to their respective ordinary occupations."—*Cyclopedia of Biblical Literature*, art. Lord's Day.

Heylyn bears witness concerning St. Chrysostom, that he—

"Confessed it to be lawful for a man to look unto his worldly business on the Lord's day, after the congregation was dismissed."—*History of the Sabbath*, part 2, chap. 3, sec. 9.

St. Jerome, in his commendation of the very pious lady Paula, speaks thus of Sunday labor :—

"Paula, with the women, as soon as they returned home on the Lord's day, they sat down severally to their work, and made clothes for themselves and others."—*Dialogues on the Lord's Day*, p. 234.

The bishop of Ely thus testifies :—

"In St. Jerome's days, and in the very place where he was residing, the devoutest Christians did ordinarily work upon the Lord's day, when the service of the church was ended."—*Treatise of the Sabbath Day*, p. 219.

There is a vast difference between divine and human authority. The latter cannot control the conscience as the former can. These persons knew very well that the Sunday rested upon only human authority. It was a gradual process, taking quite a space of time before Sunday gained the position it now holds. Dr. Heylyn bears the following testimony concerning the status of Sunday during the fifth and sixth centuries :—

"The faithful being united better than before, became more uniform in matters of devotion ; and in that uniformity did agree together to give the Lord's day all the honors of an holy festival. Yet was not this done all at once, but by degrees, the fifth and sixth centuries being wellnigh spent before it came into that hight which hath since continued. The emperors and the prelates in these times had the same affections ; both [being] earnest to advance this day above all other ; and to the edicts of the one, and ecclesiastical constitutions of the other, it stands indebted for many of those privileges and exemptions which it still enjoyeth."—*History of the Sabbath*, part 2, chap. 4, sec. 1

Here we see the same solicitude in behalf of Sunday on the part of the "prelates" of the church, which has appeared all along since apostasy and corruption first entered after the days of the apostles. "*They were earnest to advance the day above all other.*" This change of the Sabbath was really the work of the Roman Catholic Church. It was this that influenced the emperors and civil rulers. There was one honor, however, still belonging to the seventh day, which Sunday had not acquired. Thus the bishop of Ely says :—

"When the ancient Fathers distinguish and give proper names to the particular days of the week, they always style the Saturday, '*Sabbatum,* the Sabbath,' and the Sunday, or first day of the week, '*Dominicum,* the Lord's day.'"—*Treatise of the Sabbath Day*, p. 202.

This statement, however, must not be taken as referring to an earlier writer than Tertullian. He first called it the Lord's day about A. D. 200. It is doubtless true of the later Fathers.

Brerewood says :—

"The name of the Sabbath remained appropriated to the old Sabbath, and was never attributed to the Lord's day, not of many hundred years after our Saviour's time."—*Learned Treatise of the Sabbath*, p. 73. Edition 1631.

Dr. Heylyn says of the term "Sabbath" in the ancient church :—

"The Saturday is called among them by no other name than that which formerly it had, the *Sabbath*. So that whenever for a thousand years and upwards, we meet with *Sabbatum* in any writer of what name soever, it must be understood of no day but *Saturday*."—*History of the Sabbath*, part 2, chap. 2, sec. 12.

Again he says :—

"The first who ever used it to denote the Lord's day (the first that I have met with in all this search) is one Petrus Alfonsus—he lived about the time that Rupertus did [which was the beginning of the twelfth century]—who calls the Lord's day by the name of Christian Sabbath."—*Idem*, part 2, chap. 5, sec. 13.

This is a striking fact which should never be forgotten in the investigation of this question. It was not until the middle of the Dark Ages that Sunday was ever called the Sabbath. The ancient Sabbath retained its own distinctive title for eleven hundred years after Christ, and no other day during all this period was known by this title but the seventh day. Not an instance can be found in history to the contrary.

Sunday steadily advanced in popular favor down to the beginning of the sixth century, becoming the usual day on which public meetings were held, and at least a partial rest day, but had never yet been called the Sabbath.

The next six or seven centuries from this time was an age of great barbarism and spiritual darkness. Men's minds were controlled by the grossest superstitions. The power of the popes was almost supreme. Not one person in a hundred could read or write, and books were very few and expensive. The Bible was banished from the hands of the common people, and nearly every copy was in either Greek or Latin, languages which at this time were not spoken by the masses. Very few persons, comparatively, ever saw a Bible. During a part of this time, it was considered a great crime for a common person to be found reading the Bible, and the offense was punishable by the Inquisition.

It is not necessary that we should carefully note the steps by which Sunday attained to a higher power in such an age. We have already seen how, step by step, it stealthily advanced until that time, first asking only toleration, next claiming equality with the ancient Sabbath, and then taking a position above it as a joyous day, while the latter was made a fast day. Afterward it was called the Lord's day of apostolic times. Finally it was advanced by heathen emperor and Roman pope to the dignity of a day of partial rest. It cast the creation Sabbath aside by Catholic counsel, declaring that all who observed it were heretics, and placed them under a curse ; and lastly, it was sustained by popes, emperors, and councils, claiming the whole field as its own.

From this time forward, at every convenient occasion, a Catholic council would put forth a canon in behalf of the "venerable day of the sun," striving to make the people observe it more sacredly. It would weary the mind of the reader were we to give a list of all these, and what they said concerning this pet institution of the church of Rome. We will, however, mention a few of the Roman Catholic councils. The first Council of Orleans, A. D. 507, "obliged themselves and successors to be always at the church on the Lord's day." The third Council of Orleans, A. D. 538, required agricultural labor to be laid aside on the Lord's day, "in order that the people may not be prevented from attending church." In 538 another council was held in Mascon, a town in Burgundy, because "Christian people very much neglect and slight the Lord's day," giving themselves to common work, etc. The bishops warned them against such practices, and commanded them to keep the Lord's day. About a year later another council was held in Narbonne, which forbade all persons from doing any work on the Lord's day, on penalty of a "fine if a freeman," or of "being lashed if a servant." In 654 one was held at Chalons, another in England in 692, also one in 747, one in Bavaria in 772, again one in England in 784. Five councils were called by Charlemagne in the year 813, and one was held in Rome in 826. In all of these, strong efforts were made to build up the Sunday sacredness. Many others were also held for the same purpose.

But as these laws failed to accomplish all that the Catholics desired, and Sunday was still but poorly kept, they had recourse to miracles,— a very popular argument with the Romish Church. Gregory of Tours, A. D. 570, furnishes several. A husbandman went out to plow on the Lord's day, and trying to clean his plow with an iron, "the iron stuck fast to his hand for two years, . . . to his exceeding great pain and shame." Some were killed by lightning for working on that day. Others were seized with convulsions. Apparitions appeared to kings, charging them to enforce Sunday sacredness. A miller was at one time grinding corn on Sunday, and instead of the usual production of meal, a torrent of blood came forth. At another time a woman was trying to bake her bread upon this venerable day, but upon putting it in the oven, it remained only dough. It was said of the souls in purgatory that on every —

"Lord's day they were manumitted from their pains, and fluttered up and down the lake Avernus in the shape of birds." — *Heylyn's History of the Sabbath*, part 2, chap. 5, sec. 2.

It seems a little strange to us to read of such things; but these were regarded as sober facts by the historians of those times, and as strong arguments for Sunday sacredness. We must not fail to mention the roll "which came down from heaven," in which the first authority from Christ is found in behalf of Sunday. The one great lack hitherto had been divine authority for it. None was claimed by the early Fathers. "Tradition" and "custom," as we have seen, were all the authority for it which could be found until emperors and popes added theirs. But even in those dark ages the want of something more was needed. Council after council was held to enforce it, yet the people were not so impressed by them that they would wholly refrain from labor on the venerable Sunday. Something more must be obtained.

In the year 1200, Eustace, the abbot of Flaye, in Normandy, came to England, and labored very ardently in behalf of Sunday. But meeting with opposition in his efforts, he returned to Normandy. Although repulsed, he did not abandon the contest. After remaining there about a year, he returned with this remarkable roll. It was entitled—

" THE HOLY COMMANDMENT AS TO THE LORD'S DAY,

"Which came from heaven to Jerusalem, and was found upon the altar of Saint Simeon, in Golgotha, where Christ was crucified for the sins of the world. The Lord sent down this epistle, which was found upon the altar of Saint Simeon, and after looking upon which three days and three nights, some men fell upon the earth, imploring mercy of God. And after the third hour, the patriarch arose, and Acharias, the archbishop, and they opened the scroll, and received the holy epistle from God. And when they had taken the same, they found this writing therein :—

"'I am the Lord who commanded you to observe the holy day of the Lord, and ye have not kept it, and have not repented of your sins, as I have said in my gospel, "Heaven and earth shall pass away, but my words shall not pass away." Whereas I cause to be preached unto you repentance and amendment of life, you did not believe me, I have sent against you the pagans, who have shed your blood on the earth ; and yet you have not believed; and because you did not keep the Lord's day holy, for a few days you suffered hunger, but soon I gave you fullness, and after that you did still worse again. Once more, it is my will that no one from the ninth hour on Saturday until sunrise on Monday, shall do any work except that which is good.

"'And if any person shall do so, he shall with penance make amends for the same. And if you do not pay obedience to this command, verily I say unto you, and I swear unto you, by my seat, and by my throne, and by the cherubim who watch my holy seat, that I will give you my commands by no other epistle, but I will open the heavens, and for rain I will rain upon you stones, and wood, and hot water in the night, that no one may take precautions against the same, and so that I may destroy all wicked men.

"'This do I say unto you; for the Lord's holy day, you shall die the death; and for the other festivals of my saints which you have not kept, I will send unto you beasts that have the heads of lions, the hair of women, the tails of camels, and they shall be so ravenous that they shall devour your flesh, and you shall long to flee away to the tombs of the dead, and to hide yourselves for fear of the beasts; and I will take away the light of the sun from before your eyes, and will send darkness upon you, that not seeing, you may slay one another, and that I may remove from you my face, and may not show mercy upon you. For I will burn the bodies and the hearts of you, and of all those who do not keep as holy the day of the Lord.'" (See Andrews's "History of the Sabbath," second edition, pp. 386–389; Matthew Paris's "Historia Major," pp. 200, 201, edition 1640; Heylyn's "History of the Sabbath," part 2, chap. 7, sec. 5; Morer's "Lord's Day," pp. 288–290; Gilfillan's "The Sabbath," p. 399, and many others.)

We have given over one half of this famous document, which in view of our brief space, will perhaps suffice. That such a document was actually brought to England at the time mentioned, and used with strong effect to enforce the observance of Sunday, does not admit of any doubt. It is substantiated by all the reliable historians of that age. To read such a document in this skeptical age, may appear to us a little ludicrous. But at the time it was written, the hight of the Dark Ages, it was far different. That was the age of relics, —an age when a nail or a piece of wood of the true cross was of inestimable value; when the bones, toe nails, and other mementoes of the saints were considered of the highest worth. The credulity of the people knew no bounds, and the Romish priests took every advantage of it. It was by such means as this that support was supplied and holiness ascribed to the "venerable day of the sun." There is no question but that this remarkable document came from the pope himself. This is stated on the authority of Matthew Paris, whom Dr. Murdock says "is accounted the best historian of the Middle Ages,—learned, independent, honest, and judicious." Mosheim also says that the first place was due to him as "a writer of the highest merit."

This writer says :—

"But when the patriarch and clergy of all the Holy Land had diligently examined the contents of this epistle, it was decreed in a general deliberation that the epistle should be sent to the judgment of the Roman pontiff, seeing that whatever he decreed to be done, would please all. And when at length the epistle had come to the knowledge of the lord pope, immediately he ordained heralds, who, being sent through different parts of the world, preached everywhere the doctrine of this epistle, . . . among whom the abbott of Flay, Eustachius by name, a devout and learned man, having entered the kingdom of England, did there shine with many miracles."—*Matthew Paris's Historia Major*, p. 201.

Innocent III. was pope at that time, and no pontiff that ever sat in the papal chair exceeded him in efforts to elevate and strengthen the popish power. It was by such steps as these that the Romish Church advanced the interests of Sunday. Custom, tradition, the edicts of emperors, popes, and councils, counterfeit miracles, and rolls manufactured by priestly craft, and palmed off, as of heavenly origin, upon the ignorant, bigoted, and credulous multitude by the sanction of the pope and higher prelates,—these are the foundations upon which the Sunday Sabbath rests.

It is stated by historians that the Lord's day was better observed because of this second roll, and the work of this zealous abbot in England. It had, doubtless, a strong influence in many places in that superstitious age. Having thus traced the Sunday down to the middle of the Dark Ages, we will next notice it in the time of the Reformation.

CHAPTER XVI.

ATTITUDE OF THE REFORMERS TOWARD SUNDAY.

THE design of this treatise is principally to give a brief, connected view of the change of the Sabbath, and not to say all that can be said on the subject, or even present many things which would be of interest to an inquiring mind concerning the Sabbath question. And though the position the reformers took in relation to the first day of the week is not directly connected with the main object of these articles, we cannot forego a brief chapter on this subject. Our investigation of the rise of Sunday to prominence as a sacred day in the church, has thus far been wholly connected with the apostasy, which finally fully developed into the papacy. The rise of Sunday kept even pace with the work of corruption in the church, so that the highest point of Romish apostasy was contemporary with the highest degree of Sunday sacredness. The inquiring reader will be anxious to know what ground the great reformers took relative to this institution. We will answer but briefly, as our space is limited.

The great Reformation of the sixteenth century arose in the bosom of the Catholic Church itself. Many of the reformers were priests of that church before the Reformation commenced. All of them had been trained up in its communion, and were accustomed to observe its festivals, and had, at first, full respect for its authority. They were, in short, good Catholics when they began the work of reform. From their earliest infancy they had reverenced the institutions of the church, and at first never dreamed of leaving the church or of rebelling against the pope. They doubtless would have remained in the bosom of the church had they not been so pressed by their enemies, that, driven to the wall, they had to take their stand.

Under such circumstances it could not be expected that these men in that age of reverence for the hoary past would be able to see all the errors into which the church had drifted, or come back at once to the complete purity of apostolic religion. These men are deserving of high honor for the great advance out of darkness which they did make, and God greatly blessed their labors. But reformation since their time has still continued, and doubtless will till the close of time. No men of any one generation are entitled to all the credit for the blessed light of our age. It has been gradually dawning.

Mosheim well says :—

"The vindicators of religious liberty do not discover all truth in an instant, but like persons emerging from long darkness, their vision improves gradually."

Dean Stanley says :—

"Each age of the church has, as it were, turned over a new leaf in the Bible, and found a response to its own wants."—*History of the Eastern Church*, p. 79, ed. 1872.

The Protestants of the present day would not accept all that the early reformers believed. It is well known that Martin Luther and many others held fast to the doctrine of consubstantiation, that is, that the actual flesh and blood of Christ were in the consecrated bread and wine of the Lord's supper, after the priest had blessed it. Many things were held and tolerated which we would not now think consistent. It causes no surprise, therefore, that most of the reformers did not see all the truth of God's word concerning the ancient Sabbath. After a thousand years of such gross darkness, while tradition was generally reckoned to be of supreme authority, this would have been too much to expect.

ATTITUDE OF THE REFORMERS. 145

But what was the position taken by them concerning Sunday sacredness? Did they regard it as the day which Christ had set apart as the Christian Sabbath? Did they consider there was any scriptural authority for it? that it was sin to do ordinary work upon it? or that there was any command of God that it should be kept holy? Or did they consider it merely a festival day, like Christmas, Good Friday, or other days appointed by the church? We quote as follows :—

"In the Augsburg Confession, which was drawn up by Melancthon [and approved by Luther], to the question, 'What ought we to think of the Lord's day?' it is answered that the Lord's day, Easter, Whitsuntide, and other such holy days ought to be kept, *because they are appointed by the church*, that all things may be done in order; but that the observance of them is not to be thought necessary to salvation, nor the violation of them, if it be done without offense to others, to be regarded as a sin."—*Cox's Sabbath Laws*, p. 287.

The Confession of the Swiss churches says on this point :—

"The observance of the Lord's day is founded not on any commandment of God, but on the authority of the church; and the church may alter the day at pleasure."
—*Idem*.

Tyndale, the great English reformer, said :—

"As for the Sabbath, we be lords over the Sabbath, and may yet change it into Monday, or into any other day as we see need, or may make every tenth day holy day only if we see cause why!"—*Tyndale's Answer to More*, book 1, chap. 25.

Zwingle, the great Swiss reformer, regarded it thus :—

"For we are no way bound to time, but time ought so to serve us, that it is lawful, and permitted to each church, when necessity urges (as is usual to be done in harvest time), to transfer the solemnity and rest of the Lord's day, or Sabbath, to some other day."—*Hessey*, p. 352.

John Calvin said respecting the Sunday festival:—

"However, the ancients have not without sufficient reason substituted what we call the Lord's day in the room of the Sabbath. . . . Yet I do not lay so much stress on the septenary number that I would oblige the church to an invariable adherence to it; nor will I condemn those churches which have other solemn days for their assemblies, provided they keep at a distance from superstition."—*Calvin's Institutes of the Christian Religion*, translated by John Allen, book 2, chap. 8, sec. 34.

These words from Calvin, the founder of the Presbyterian Church, the strictest observers of Sunday, perhaps, of any denomination, may surprise many. But we shall find that their views of Sunday strictness were of later origin. Certainly Calvin did not share in them; for it seems he himself was not particularly strict as a Sunday-keeper. Dr. Hessey says:—

"Knox, the intimate friend of Calvin, visited Calvin, and, it is said, on one occasion found him enjoying the recreation of bowls on Sunday."—*Hessey's Bampton Lectures on Sunday*, p. 201. Edition 1866.

Calvin had Servetus arrested on Sunday. John Barclay, a learned man of Scotch descent, whose early life was spent near Geneva, published the statement that Calvin and his friends at Geneva—

"Debated whether the reformed, for the purpose of estranging themselves more completely from the Romish

Church, should not adopt Thursday as the Christian Sabbath," one reason assigned by Calvin being, "that it would be a proper instance of Christian liberty."

These statements have been credited by many learned Protestants, and we are not aware that they have ever been disproved. Knox was not such a believer in the sacredness of Sunday as Presbyterians now are. Thus we see the leading reformers were not believers in Sunday sacredness, as many modern Protestants are. They considered it a church festival, and not as receiving its authority from the fourth commandment.

Carlstadt, the German reformer, kept the seventh-day Sabbath. He was a leading reformer, one who went farther in opposition to the Roman Church than Luther and many others. His position was in some respects more consistent than Luther's. He insisted on rejecting everything in the Catholic Church not authorized by the Scriptures, while Luther was determined to retain everything not expressly forbidden. Had Carlstadt's position been taken, the Protestant church would have come much nearer the truth of the Bible on the Sabbath question than it has.

Many will doubtless be surprised at these evidences of the low regard these early reformers had for the Sunday Sabbath, admitting, as they did, that it was wholly an institution of the church, and not required in the Scriptures. It is well known that this is not now the general position of many of the Protestant churches. They consider Sunday the Sabbath by divine appointment, and would highly resent such sentiments as history records concerning the opinions of the leading reformers. Some may doubt the truthfulness of these statements; but we assure them that there are no facts better attested, and that we could present much evidence on this point substantiating what we have already said. The real facts are these: In the great controversy in England between the Episcopalians and the Presbyterians, in the latter part of the sixteenth century, as the latter rejected the authority of the church and most of its festivals, while the Episcopalians required men to observe all the festivals of the church, it was clearly seen that in order to maintain the authority of Sunday, which the Presbyterians kept, they must find some other arguments in its behalf than those which had sustained it for so many ages. They had therefore either to give up Sunday, or try to find arguments for it in the Bible. They chose the latter course.

Lyman Coleman, a first-day historian, thus states the promulgation of the modern opinion :—

"The true doctrine of the Christian Sabbath was first promulgated by an English dissenter, the Rev. Nicholas Bound, D. D., of Norton, in the county of Suffolk. About the year 1595 he published a famous book, entitled 'Sabbathum Veteris et Novi Testamenti,' or the 'True Doctrine of the Sabbath.' In this book he maintained 'that the seventh part of our time ought to be devoted to God; that Christians are bound to rest on the Lord's day as much as the Jews were on the Mosaic Sabbath, the commandment about rest being moral and perpetual; and that it was not lawful for persons to follow their studies or worldly business on that day, nor to use such pleasures and recreations as are permitted on other days.' This book spread with wonderful rapidity. The doctrine which is propounded called forth from many hearts a ready response, and the result was a most pleasing reformation in many parts of the kingdom. 'It is almost incredible,' says Fuller, 'how taking this doctrine was, partly because of its own purity, and partly for the eminent piety of such persons as maintained it; so that the Lord's day, especially in corporations, began to be precisely kept; people becoming a law unto themselves, forbearing such sports as yet by statutes permitted; yea, many rejoicing at their own restraint herein.'"—*Coleman's Ancient Christianity Exemplified*, chap. 26, sec. 2.

This new doctrine "spread with wonderful rapidity," and has since been substantially adopted by many of the Protestant churches, but not by all. It is now the popular doctrine of the change of the Sabbath which is generally held. Scattered hints of this doctrine in parts had been held before by a few; but it never had been put forth as a whole in the form of a system. During some fourteen centuries of first-day Sabbath agitation, such a doctrine had never been promulgated. The Christian Fathers, to whom Sunday elevation is remotely traced, never heard of such a doctrine. The change they wrought was for an entirely different reason. It was founded upon "custom," "tradition," "voluntary choice," but never upon any Bible authority, never upon the fourth commandment.

Of all the arrogant, preposterous claims—and they have been many—put forth in behalf of the "venerable day of the sun," the most preposterous is reserved for the last,—that of claiming for it the authority of the fourth commandment. It took some fourteen centuries to invent this claim, so contrary to the Bible record. If it is not "stealing the livery of heaven," for the first day of the week to shield itself under and clothe itself with the commandment of God,—"Remember the Sabbath day to keep it holy," "the seventh day is the Sabbath of the Lord thy God,"—then we know not what would be. The command requiring us to observe the day of Jehovah's rest which he blessed and set apart for a sacred use at the creation of the world, for man to keep ever holy, is now sanctimoniously appropriated to bolster up another day entirely, the one on which he commenced his work of creation. We do not know how mortal man could go farther in doing despite to the rest of the great God.

Here is where first-day observers have intrenched themselves for some two hundred years past. Here is where we find them to-day. The great heathen "memorial" of idolatry intrenched in the sacred temple of the memorial of the Creator! The first day of the week claiming as its fundamental authority the commandment of God which was given to enforce the observance of the seventh day, an entirely different day!

Well does J. N. Andrews say concerning this last step taken to save Sunday:—

"Such was the origin of the seventh-part-of-time theory, by which the seventh day is dropped out of the fourth commandment, and one day in seven slipped into its place,—a doctrine most opportunely framed at the very period when nothing else could save the venerable day of the sun. With the aid of this theory, the Sunday of 'pope and pagan' was able coolly to wrap itself in the fourth commandment, and then, in the character of a divine institution, to challenge obedience from all Bible Christians. It could not cast away the other frauds on which its very existence had depended, and support its authority by this one alone. In the time of Constantine it ascended the throne of the Roman empire, and during the whole period of the Dark Ages it maintained its supremacy from the chair of St. Peter; but now it had ascended to the throne of the Most High. And thus a day which God 'commanded not nor spake it, neither came it into' his 'mind,' was enjoined upon mankind with all the authority of his holy law."— *Andrews's History of the Sabbath*, pp. 479, 480.

CHAPTER XVII.

TRACES OF THE SABBATH WHERE THE CATHOLIC CHURCH COULD NOT SUPPRESS IT.

HAVING traced the Sunday Sabbath from its first beginnings through the Dark Ages to its full adoption by the Protestant churches, we now return to the true Sabbath, to notice briefly its status since the Roman Catholic Church caused it to be discontinued where it had the power to do so. It will be remembered that we gave clear proof that it was kept in the early church for centuries, even till the Catholic Council of Laodicea, in A. D. 364, abrogated it by an anathema. From that time forward it gradually disappeared from view in those countries where the Catholic Church had supreme influence. That church has made the most persistent efforts, in every way possible, to crush out the ancient Sabbath, seeming to realize that those who clung to it struck at the very foundation of her claims.

Sunday stands upon the authority of tradition; the Sabbath stands upon the authority of the commandments of God. When Sunday is observed, one really recognizes the groundwork of Catholic authority, viz., tradition, and, logically speaking, would be bound to accept her other festivals, ordinances, etc., which stand on precisely the same authority. But when a person ignores Sunday and keeps the Sabbath of the Lord, he sets aside every scrap of Catholic tradition, so that the whole Catholic stock in trade is gone, together with their strongest hold on Protestants. Hence we shall ever find Catholics stoutly opposed to the Sabbath.

We shall now inquire whether the Sabbath did not continue to be observed in various places where the Roman Church had not influence enough to suppress it. If this be so, it will afford strong additional evidence that the change of the Sabbath was wrought by the power of the Catholic Church. We shall be able to give only brief historical references in proof of this point, referring those who wish to investigate the matter thoroughly to the work before noticed, Andrews's "History of the Sabbath," a much more complete treatise than this can be.

We first notice the early Christians of Great Britain who were not connected with Rome before the mission of Augustine in A. D. 596. These were a pious, humble class of people, and were in an eminent degree Bible Christians.

"An Irish presbyter, Columba, feeling himself stirred with missionary zeal, and doubtless knowing the wretched condition of the savage Scots and Picts in the year 565, took with him twelve other missionaries, and passed over to Scotland."—*M'Clintock and Strong's Cyclopedia*, vol. 2, p. 601.

They were called Culdees, and settled and made their head-quarters on the little isle of Iona. They had, for the most part, "a simple and primitive form of Christianity," very different from the pomp of Romanism.

Two eminent Catholic authors speak of Columba as follows :—

"Having continued his labors in Scotland thirty-four years, he clearly and openly foretold his death, and on Saturday, the ninth of June, said to his disciple Diermit, 'This day is called the Sabbath, that is, the day of rest, and such will it truly be to me; for it will put an end to my labors.'"—*Butler's Lives of the Fathers, Martyrs, and Principal Saints*, art. St. Columba, A. D. 597.

"To-day is Saturday, the day which the Holy Scriptures call the Sabbath, or rest. And it will truly be my day of rest, for it shall be the last of my laborious life."—*The Monks of the West*, vol. 2, p. 104.

This language proves that Columba believed that Saturday was the true Bible Sabbath. It also shows his satisfaction in the fact, in view of his immediate death. We have never known an observer of Sunday to have any feelings of pleasure on his death-bed in view of the fact that Saturday was the Bible Sabbath. Hence we conclude that this man of God, the leader of these missionaries, was an observer of the ancient Sabbath.

There had been no class of dissenters from the Catholic Church more worthy of regard than the Waldenses, or Vaudois, whose principal settlement was in the valleys of the Alps in Piedmont, though at times there were companies of them scattered in many of the countries of Europe Their locating in these valleys occurred between the time of Constantine and the full development of the Roman Catholic Church. There is some confusion as to the exact time among the various authorities. It seems to be a settled fact among historians that the cause of their seeking these retired valleys was their desire to maintain the purity of their religion, and to escape the corrupting influences so prevalent in the more thickly populated portions of the country. So they retired from public view. They had a translation of the Bible in their own tongue, and taught it with great diligence to their children. Catholic writers declare that some of them could repeat nearly the whole of the Holy Scriptures. They sent out missionaries to all parts of Europe during the darkest days of the papacy. Many of these witnessed for the truth with their lives. Multitudes of them died in the various persecutions by the Catholics. Time after time they were driven from their homes into the mountains and caves, and many thousands of men, women, and children were put to death, and their property and homes confiscated and destroyed.

There is conclusive evidence that a portion, at least, of the Waldenses observed the ancient Sabbath in the days of their greatest purity. A considerable portion of this people were called by the significant designation of *Sabbati*, *Sabbatati*, or *Insabbatati*. Mr. Robinson, the historian, quotes out of Gretser the words of Goldastus, as follows:—

"Insabbatati [they were called] not because they were circumcised, but because they kept the Jewish Sabbath."—*Ecclesiastical Researches*, chap. 10, p. 303.

Goldastus was a learned Swiss historian and jurist, who was born in 1576. He was a Calvinist writer of note. Archbishop Usher acknowledges that many understood they were called by these names because they kept the Jewish Sabbath, though he thought it was for another reason.

Just before the great Protestant Reformation,—

"Louis XII., king of France, being informed by the enemies of the Waldenses inhabiting a part of the province of Provence, that several heinous crimes were laid to their account, sent the Master of Requests and a certain doctor of the Sorbonne, who was confessor to His Majesty, to make inquiry into the matter. On their return they reported that they had visited all the parishes where they dwelt, had inspected their places of worship, but they had found there no images nor signs of the ornaments belonging to the mass nor any of the ceremonies of the Romish Church ; much less could they discover any traces of those crimes with which they were charged. On the contrary, they kept the Sabbath day, observed the ordinance of baptism according to the primitive church, instructed their children in the articles of the Christian faith and the commandments of God. The king, having read the report of his commissioners, said with an oath that they were better men than himself or his people."—*Jones's Church History*, vol. 2, chap. 5, sec. 4.

"The respectable French historian De Thou says that the Vaudois keep the commandments of the decalogue, and allow among them of no wickedness, detesting perjuries, imprecations, quarrels, seditions, etc."—*History of the Vaudois*, by Bresse, p. 126.

One portion of the Waldenses were called Passaginians, probably because they lived high up in the passes of the Alps. Thus Mosheim speaks of them:—

"In Lombardy, which was the principal residence of the Italian heretics, there sprung up a singular sect, known, for what reason I cannot tell, by the denomination of Passaginians, and also by that of the Circumcised. Like the other sects already mentioned, they had the utmost aversion to the dominion and discipline of the church of Rome; but they were at the same time distinguished by two religious tenets which were peculiar to themselves The first was a notion that the observance of the law of Moses in everything except the offering of sacrifices, was obligatory upon Christians; in consequence of which they circumcised their followers, abstained from those meats the use of which was prohibited unter the Mosaic economy, and celebrated the Jewish Sabbath."—*Ecclesiastical History*, cent. 12, part 2, chap. 5, sec 14.

But Mr. Benedict, in his "History of the Baptist Denomination," speaks of them as follows:—

"The account of their practicing circumcision is undoubtedly a slanderous story, forged by their enemies, and probably arose in this way: Because they observed the seventh day, they were called, by way of derision, Jews, as the Sabbatarians are frequently at this day; and if they were Jews, it followed, of course, that they either did, or ought to, circumcise their followers. This was probably the reasoning of their enemies; but that they actually practiced the bloody rite is altogether improbable."—Vol. 2, p. 414. Edition 1813.

Such has ever been the conduct of the Romish Church—to blacken the character of its enemies by false reports. It is nothing uncommon at the present day for even Protestant ministers to make such charges upon Sabbatarians—that they are Jews, and keep all the law of Moses, because they observe the Sabbath. They might know, if they cared to, that Sabbatarians make a great distinction between the moral law of ten commandments, which requires the observance of the seventh-day Sabbath, and the ceremonial law of types, shadows, circumcision, etc. The former they believe to be binding on all; the latter was abolished at the cross of Christ.

The Petrobrusians were a sect of French Christians who, in the twelfth century, witnessed for God in opposition to the papacy. They were also observers of the Sabbath. This is stated by Dr. Francis White, lord bishop of Ely, who was appointed by the king of England to write against the Sabbath in opposition to Mr. Brabourne, a Sabbatarian. He says:—

"In St. Bernard's days it was condemned in the Petrobruysans."—*Treatise of the Sabbath Day*, p. 8.

The Sabbath-keepers of the eleventh century were of sufficient importance to attract the attention of the pope. Gregory VII., one of the most lordly, domineering popes that ever occupied the papal chair, was at that time ruling the church with an iron hand. Dr. Heylyn says that—

"Gregory, of that name the seventh [about A. D. 1074], condemned those who taught that it was not lawful to do work on the day of the Sabbath."—*History of the Sabbath*, part 2, chap. 5, sec. 1.

This is clear evidence that there was still a respectable number of Sabbath-keepers, even in those countries where that church had authority; for surely the pope would not pronounce a curse upon them unless such persons existed. Thus we see the Sabbath still existing among those opposed to the Catholic Church, even in Italy itself, where the pope's power was greatest. We now look abroad to countries where the pope never had jurisdiction, in search of those who still revere the Sabbath of the Lord.

The gospel extended its influence all through Northern and Central Africa in the early part of the Christian dispensation. There were many Christian churches on that continent. Africa indeed "stretched out her hands to God." But after the conquest of the northern portions of that country by the Mohammedans, and for a long time before that, the Christians of Abyssinia were lost to the rest of the Christian world. Says Gibbon:—

"Encompassed on all sides by the enemies of their religion, the Ethiopians slept near a thousand years, forgetful of the world, by whom they were forgotten."— *Decline and Fall*, chap. 47, par. 38.

But after the great discoveries of the fifteenth and sixteenth centuries, they became known again to the Christian world. They were found observing the ancient Sabbath, although they were greatly affected by the pagan and Mohammedan errors so long surrounding them, as might be expected. Yet it is a fact of no little significance in the consideration of this subject, that this large body of Christians, which had been so long separated from the influence of the Catholic Church, were found after a thousand years still observing the seventh day. At the time of their separation from the rest of the Christian world, they, with others, were observing both Sunday and the Sabbath. When found nearly a thousand years later, they were doing the same, as Mr. Geddes says :—

"They deny purgatory, and know nothing of confirmation and extreme unction; they condemn graven images; they keep both Saturday and Sunday."—*Church History of Ethiopia*, pp. 34, 35.

The ambassador of the king of Ethiopia, at the court of Lisbon, gave the following reasons for keeping the Sabbath :—

"Because God, after he had finished the creation of the world, rested thereon; which day, as God would have it called the holy of holies, so the not celebrating thereof with great honor and devotion seems to be plainly contrary to God's will and precept, who will suffer heaven and earth to pass away sooner than his word; and that, especially, since Christ came not to destroy the law, but to fulfill it. It is not, therefore, in imitation of the Jews, but in obedience to Christ and his holy apostles, that we observe that day."—*Church History of Ethiopia*, pp. 87, 88.

This account was given by the ambassador in 1534. In the beginning of the next century the emperor of Abyssinia was induced to submit to the pope in these words :—

"I confess that the pope is the vicar of Christ, the successor of St. Peter, and the sovereign of the world. To him I swear true obedience, and at his feet I offer my person and kingdom."—*Gibbon's Decline and Fall of the Roman Empire*, chap. 47, par. 39.

Let the reader now mark what followed: As soon as the emperor had thus submitted himself, he was obliged to put forth a decree forbidding the observance of the Sabbath. Geddes says he—

"Set forth a proclamation prohibiting all his subjects, upon severe penalties, to observe Saturday any longer."
—*Church History of Ethiopia*, pp. 311, 312.

Gibbon expresses the edict thus :—

"The Abyssinians were enjoined to work and to play on the Sabbath."—*Decline and Fall*, chap. 47, par. 39.

Thus we see the Roman Church never missed a chance to give the ancient Sabbath a thrust when the opportunity presented itself. This one desire has marked its course throughout. After a space of time the tyranny of the Catholics brought a terrible struggle, which caused their overthrow, and the Abyssinians returned to the observance of the Sabbath, and have continued to do so ever since. These facts present a striking evidence of the hatred of the Roman Church toward the Sabbath. It also conclusively proves the existence of the Sabbath in the church where the popish power could not abrogate it.

We next notice the Armenians of the East Indies. Here was quite a large body of Christians who had little or no connection with the churches of Europe for many centuries. So they were preserved from many of the false doctrines of the great apostasy. Mr. Massie describes them as follows :—

"Separated from the Western world for a thousand years, they were naturally ignorant of many novelties introduced by the councils and decrees of the Lateran; and *their conformity with the faith and practice of the first ages* laid them open to the unpardonable guilt of heresy and schism, as estimated by the church of Rome. 'We are Christians, and not idolaters,' was their expressive reply when required to do homage to the image of the Virgin Mary. . . . La Croze states them at fifteen hundred churches, and as many towns and villages. They refused to recognize the pope, and declared they had never heard of him; they asserted the purity and primitive truth of their faith since they came, and their bishops had for thirteen hundred years been sent, from the place where the followers of Jesus were first called Christians."—*Continental India*, vol. 2, pp. 116, 117.

Mr. Yeates hints at the Sabbatarian character of these Christians. He says that Saturday—

"Among them is a festival day, *agreeable to the ancient practice of the church.*"—*East Indian Church History*, pp. 133, 134.

The same fact is also again hinted at by the same writer as follows :—

"The Inquisition was set up at Goa in the Indies, at the instance of Francis Xaverius [a famous Romish saint], who signified by letters to the Pope John III., Nov. 10, 1545, 'That THE JEWISH WICKEDNESS spreads more and more in the parts of the East Indies subject to the kingdom of Portugal, and therefore he earnestly besought the said king, that to cure so great an evil he would take care to send the office of the Inquisition into those countries.'"—*Idem*, pp. 139, 140

There can be no reasonable doubt that the "Jewish wickedness" here referred to is the same as observing Saturday "agreeable to the ancient practice of the church," spoken of above. We here have another evidence of the hatred of the Roman Church to the Sabbath. It must be put down by the Inquisition, if found in existence where that church had authority. Since that time the East Indies have fallen under the dominion of Great Britain. Some years since, Mr. Buchanan, a distinguished minister of the Church of England, visited India for the purpose of becoming acquainted with this body of Christians. He says they have preserved themselves most free from Mohammedan and papal corruptions, and that they have a translation of the Bible in the Armenian language, which has been pronounced the "queen of versions." He says:—

"They have preserved the Bible in its purity; and their doctrines are, as far as the author knows, the doctrines of the Bible. Besides, they maintain the solemn observance of Christian worship throughout our empire ON THE SEVENTH DAY, and they have as many spires pointing to heaven among the Hindoos as we ourselves."—*Buchanan's Christian Researches in Asia*, p. 259.

Purchas, a writer of the seventeenth century, also speaks of several sects of Eastern Christians, "continuing from ancient times," as Syrians, Jacobites, Nestorians, Maronites, and Armenians. It seems evident that these are identical with those now known as Armenians. He says:—

"They keep Saturday holy, nor esteem Saturday fast lawful but on Easter even. They have solemn service on Saturdays, eat flesh, and feast it bravely like the Jews."—*Purchas, his Pilgrimage*, part 2, book 8, chap. 6, sec. 5.

This writer, like many first-day authors, Catholic and Protestant, even at the present time, speaks disrespectfully of those Christians who observed the Sabbath. But this testimony, with the others, seems to leave no possible doubt that the Armenians observed the Sabbath.

Andrews, in his "History of the Sabbath," page 463, says concerning other Sabbath-keepers:—

"When the Reformation had lifted the vail of darkness that covered the nations of Europe, Sabbath-keepers were found in Transylvania, Bohemia, Russia, Germany, Holland, France, and England. It was not the Reformation which gave existence to these Sabbatarians, for the leaders of the Reformation, as a body, were not friendly to such views. On the contrary, these observers of the Sabbath appear to be remnants of the ancient Sabbath-keeping churches that had witnessed for the truth during the Dark Ages."

He proceeds to cite various classes of these in the countries mentioned, and gives the authorities to prove it, which the inquiring reader can investigate in that valuable work.

In summing up the facts presented concerning these Sabbath-keeping bodies which continued through the Dark Ages, we reach the following conclusions :—

1. The Waldenses (at least a large portion of them) who sought retired places in the valleys of the mountains, to be able to worship God according to the ancient practice of the church and according to the Bible, kept the ancient Sabbath till persecuted by the Catholic Church and almost exterminated.

2. The Abyssinian Church, shut away from the papal church for a thousand years, when discovered were found observing the seventh day of the week as the early Christians did; but as soon as the Catholics got power to do so, they at once abased the Sabbath, and would not allow it to be observed while they remained in the kingdom.

3. The Armenian Christians, also shut away from the Roman Church for the same length of time, when visited by Europeans, were found keeping the seventh day, or Saturday, according to the ancient practice of

believers during the first centuries. But true to their hatred of the Sabbath, as soon as the Romish priests could do so, they had the cruel Inquisition brought in to abolish by torture the practice of keeping the ancient memorial of creation. So also was it in many other countries. It is the same old story in every instance.

We have now followed for fifteen centuries the work of the Roman Catholic Church in its continued, persevering effort to overthrow the Sabbath which God commanded, and to elevate the Sunday, the weekly memorial of sun-worship, the first form of idolatry, into its place, transforming it into a Christian institution; and we see but one purpose throughout. This work always centered at Rome, from the time the first step was taken turning the Sabbath into a fast to disgrace it, while making Sunday a joyful festival, till we reach the famous roll "which came down from heaven," threatening destruction upon those who should "fail to keep the Lord's day;" yes, continuing even till the present day, since Protestants have joined in the same work of elevating Sunday. We cannot question the fact that the papal church changed the Sabbath. But lest any should think we have unfairly judged that church in thus speaking, we propose to give the testimony of many Catholic writers themselves on this subject.

CHAPTER XVIII.

WHAT CATHOLIC AUTHORITIES SAY ABOUT THE CHANGE EFFECTED BY THEIR CHURCH.

IN considering questions of importance, like the subject under discussion, it is certainly reasonable that the parties accused should have the privilege of testifying for themselves. We have said very plainly that the papists, during the long continuance of the great apostasy, which resulted in the development of their church, have changed the Sabbath from the day which the Holy Scriptures required to another day, without the slightest Bible authority for so doing. Do they admit this charge to be true ? or do they deny it ? This is a question of real importance, one which we wish fairly and candidly to examine. We will quote Catholic authorities alone on this point.

The pope is the head of the Catholic Church; the head directs the body. The "Roman Decretalia" is an authoritative work in the Roman ecclesiastical law. Each pope, when invested with the "succession," declares the papal decretals to be true. The "Decretalia" ascribes power to the pope to change God's law or any other law. Thus :—

"He can pronounce sentences and judgments in contradiction to the right of nations, and to the law of God and man. . . . He can free himself from the commands of the apostles, he being their superior, and from the rules of the Old Testament," etc.

"The pope has power to change times, to abrogate laws, and to dispense with all things, even the precepts of Christ."—*Decretal de Translat. Episcop. Cap.*

"The pope's will stands for reason. He can dispense above the law, and of wrong make right by *correcting and changing laws.*"—*Pope Nicholas*, Dis. 96.

"The pope is free from all laws, so that he cannot incur any sentence of irregularity, suspension, excommunication, or penalty for any crime."—Dis. 40.

Surely the pope is a wonderful personage. He can be no other than the embodiment of that power which was to "think to change times and the law." Dan. 7:25. Here we see claims of plentitude of power sufficient to make any changes whatever which he might desire to make. What do papists say about changing the Sabbath? In the "Catholic Catechism of Christian Religion" we have the following questions and answers:—

"*Ques.*—What does God ordain by this commandment?

"*Ans.*—He ordains that we sanctify, in a special manner, this day on which he rested from the labor of creation.

"*Q.*—What is this day of rest?

"*A.*—The seventh day of the week, or Saturday; for he employed six days in creation, and rested on the seventh. Gen. 2:2; Heb. 4:1, etc.

"*Q.*—Is it, then, Saturday we should sanctify in order to obey the ordinance of God?

"*A.*—During the old law, Saturday was the day sanctified; *but the church*, instructed by Jesus Christ, and directed by the Spirit of God, has substituted Sunday for Saturday; so now we sanctify the first, not the seventh day. Sunday means, and now is, the day of the Lord.

"*Q.*—Had the church power to make such change?

"*A.*—Certainly; since the Spirit of God is her guide, the change is inspired by the Holy Spirit."

In another Catholic work, called the "Abridgment of Christian Doctrine," page 58, the Catholic Church asserts its power to change the law, in the following manner :—

"*Ques.*—How prove you that the church hath power to command feasts and holy days?

"*Ans.*—By the very act of changing the Sabbath into Sunday, which Protestants allow of; and therefore they fondly contradict themselves, by keeping Sunday strictly, and breaking most other feasts commanded by the same church.

"*Q.*—How prove you that?

"*A.*—Because by keeping Sunday they acknowledge the church's power to ordain feasts, and to command them under sin; and by not keeping the rest by her commanded, they again deny, in fact, the same power."

In the "Catholic Christian Instructed," p. 202, is presented the following list of feast-days, which all rest upon the same foundation, namely, the authority of the Catholic Church. Of these, Sunday takes the lead :—

"*Ques.*—What are the days which the church commands to be kept holy?

"*Ans.*—1. The Sunday, or our Lord's day, which we observe by apostolic tradition, instead of the Sabbath. 2. The feasts of our Lord's nativity, or Christmas day; his circumcision, or New Year's day; the Epiphany, or twelfth day; Easter day, or the day of our Lord's resurrection; the day of our Lord's ascension; Whitsunday, or the day of the coming of the Holy Ghost; Trinity Sunday; Corpus Christi, or the feast of the Blessed Sacrament. 3. We keep the days of the Annuciation, and Assumption of the Blessed Virgin Mary. 4. We observe the feast of All-Saints; of St. John Baptist; of the holy apostles, St. Peter and St. Paul. 5. In this kingdom [Britain-Ireland] we keep the feast of St. Patrick, our principal patron."

From pp. 202, 203 of the work last quoted, we take the following additional testimony, which also has a very important bearing on the question of the Sabbath, as the points referred to are vital ones in this issue : —

"*Ques.*—What warrant have you for keeping the Sunday preferably to the ancient Sabbath, which was the Saturday?

"*Ans.*—We have for it the authority of the Catholic Church, and apostolical tradition.

"*Q.*—Does the Scripture anywhere command the Sunday to be kept for the Sabbath?

"*A.*—The Scripture commands us to hear the church (St. Matt. 18 : 17; St. Luke 10 : 16), and to hold fast the traditions of the apostles. 2 Thess. 2 : 15. But the Scripture does not in particular mention this change of the Sabbath. St. John speaks of the Lord's day (Rev. 1 : 10); but he does not tell us what day of the week this was, much less does he tell us that this day was to take [the] place of the Sabbath ordained in the commandments. St. Luke also speaks of the disciples' meeting together to break bread on the first day of the week. Acts 20 : 7. And St. Paul (1 Cor. 16 : 2) orders that on the first day of the week the Corinthians should lay by in store what they designed to bestow in charity on the faithful in Judea; but neither the one nor the other tells us that this first day of the week was to be henceforward the day of worship, and the Christian Sabbath: so that truly, the best authority we have for this is the testimony and ordinance of the church. And therefore, those who pretend to be so religious of the Sunday, whilst they take no notice of other festivals ordained by the same church authority, show that they act by humor, and not by reason and religion; since Sundays and holydays all stand upon the same foundation; viz., the ordinance of the church."

The "Doctrinal Catechism," pp. 174, 352, offers proof that Protestants are not guided by the Scriptures. We present two of the questions and answers : —

"*Ques.*—Have you any other way of proving that the church has power to institute festivals of precept?

"*Ans.*—Had she not such power, she could not have done that in which all modern religionists agree with her,—she could not have substituted the observance of Sunday, the first day of the week, for the observance of Saturday, the seventh day, a change for which there is no scriptural authority."

"*Q.*—When Protestants do profane work upon Saturday, or the seventh day of the week, do they follow the Scripture as their only rule of faith,—do they find this permission clearly laid down in the Sacred Volume?

"*A.*—On the contrary, they have only the authority of tradition for this practice. In profaning Saturday, they violate one of God's commandments, which he has never clearly abrogated,—'Remember that thou keep holy the Sabbath day.'"

Then follows a statement and refutation of the arguments which Protestants usually rely on to prove the change of the Sabbath, such as the resurrection of Christ, the pouring out of the Spirit, the Lord's day of Rev. 1:10; Acts 20:7; and 1 Cor. 16:2, showing that these scriptures contain no evidence of the institution of Sunday observance, but that the practice rests solely upon the authority of the Catholic Church.

In a Roman Catholic work entitled "The Shortest Way to End Disputes about Religion," by the Rev. Dr. Manning, approved by the Rt. Rev. Bishop Fitzpatrick, Coadjutor of the Diocese of Boston, Mass., page 19, we find the following:—

"As zealous as Protestants are against the church's infallibility, they are forced to depend wholly upon her authority in many articles that cannot be evidently proved from any text of Scripture, yet are of very great importance.

"1. The lawfulness for Christians to work upon Saturday, contrary, in appearance, to the express command of God, who bids us 'keep the Sabbath holy,' and tells us the seventh day of the week is that day.

"2. The lawfulness and validity of infant baptism, whereof there is no example in Scripture."

In accordance with the instruction given in the catechisms from which the foregoing quotations were made, a work entitled "The Clifton Tracts" (Catholic), vol. 4, chap. 4, under the title, "A Question for all Bible Christians," makes a precise statement of the positions held respectively by Catholics and Protestants on this question, in the following forcible language: —

"I am going to propose a very plain and serious question, to which I would entreat all who profess to follow 'the Bible, and the Bible only,' to give their most earnest attention. It is this: Why do you not keep holy the Sabbath day?

"The command of Almighty God stands clearly written in the Bible in these words: 'Remember the Sabbath day, to keep it holy. Six days shalt thou labor, and do all thy work; but the seventh day is the Sabbath of the Lord thy God; in it thou shalt not do any work.' Ex. 20: 8, 9. Such being God's command, then, I ask again, Why do you not obey it? Why do you not keep holy the Sabbath day?

"You will answer me, perhaps, that you *do* keep holy the Sabbath day; for that you abstain from all worldly business, and diligently go to church, and say your prayers, and read your Bible at home, every Sunday of your lives.

"But *Sunday is not the Sabbath day;* Sunday is the *first* day of the week; the Sabbath day was the *seventh* day of the week. Almighty God did not give a commandment that men should keep holy *one day in seven;* but he named his own day, and said distinctly, Thou shalt keep holy the *seventh day;* and he assigned a reason for choosing this day rather than any other, — a reason which belongs only to the seventh day of the week, and cannot be applied to the rest. He says, 'For in six days the Lord made heaven and earth, the sea, and all that in them is, and rested the seventh day; *wherefore* the Lord blessed the Sabbath day, and hallowed it.'

"Almighty God ordered that all men should rest from their labor on the seventh day, because he too had rested on that day; he did not rest on Sunday, but on Saturday. On Sunday, which is the first day of the week, he *began* the work of creation, he did not finish it; it was on Saturday that he '*ended* his work which he had made; and he rested on the seventh day from all his work which he had made. And God blessed the seventh day, and sanctified it; because that in it he had rested from all his work which God created and made.' Gen. 2 : 2, 3. Nothing can be more plain and easy to be understood than all this, and there is nobody who attempts to deny it; it is acknowledged by everybody that the day which Almighty God appointed to be kept holy was Saturday, not Sunday. Why do you, then, keep holy the Sunday, and not the Saturday?

"You tell me that Saturday was the *Jewish* Sabbath, but that the *Christian* Sabbath has been changed to Sunday. Changed ! but by whom? Who has authority to change an express command of Almighty God? When God has spoken, and said, Thou shalt keep holy the seventh day, who shall dare to say, Nay, thou mayest work, and do all manner of worldly business on the seventh day; but thou shalt keep holy the first day in its stead? This is the most important question, which I know not how you can answer.

"You are a Protestant, and you profess to go by the Bible, and the Bible only; and yet in so important a matter as the observance of one day in seven as a holy day, you go against the plain letter of the Bible, and put another day in the place of that day which the Bible has commanded. The command to keep holy the seventh day is one of the ten commandments; you believe that the other nine are still binding; who gave you authority to tamper with the fourth? If you are consistent with your own principles, if you really follow the Bible, and the Bible only, you ought to be able to produce some portion of the New Testament in which this fourth commandment is expressly altered, or, at least, from which you may confidently infer that it was the will of God that Christians should make that change in its observance which you have made. . . .

"The present generation of Protestants keep Sunday holy instead of Saturday, because they received it as a part of the Christian religion from the last generation, and that generation received it from the generation before, and so on backward from one generation to another, by a continual succession, until we come to the time of the (so-called) Reformation, when it so happened that those who conducted the change of religion in this country, left this particular portion of Catholic faith and practice untouched.

"But, had it happened otherwise,—had some one or other of the 'reformers' taken it into his head to denounce the observance of Sunday as a popish corruption and superstition, and to insist upon it that Saturday was the day which God had appointed to be kept holy, and that he had never authorized the observance of any other, — all Protestants would have been obliged, in obedience to their professed principle of following the Bible, and the Bible only, either to acknowledge this teaching as true, and to return to the observance of the ancient Sabbath, or else to deny that there is any Sabbath at all. And so, in like manner, any one at the present day who should set about, honestly and without prejudice, to draw up for himself a form of religious belief and practice out of the written word of God, must needs come to the same conclusion; he must either believe that the Sabbath is still binding upon men's consciences, because of the divine command, Thou shalt keep holy the seventh day; or he must believe that no Sabbath at all is binding upon them, because of the apostolic injunction, Let no man judge you in respect of a festival day, or of the Sabbaths, which are a shadow of things to come, but the body is Christ's. *Either one or the other of these conclusions he might honestly come to;* but he would know nothing whatever of a *Christian* Sabbath, distinct from the ancient, celebrated on a different day and observed in a different manner, simply because Holy Scripture itself nowhere speaks of such a thing.

"Now mind, in all this you would greatly misunderstand me if you supposed I was quarreling with you for acting in this manner on a true and right principle,—in other words, a Catholic principle, viz., the acceptance, without hesitation, of that which has been handed down to you by an unbroken tradition. I would not tear from you a single one of those shreds and fragments of divine truth which you have retained. God forbid! *They are the most precious things you possess*, and by God's blessing may serve as clues to bring you out of that labyrinth of error in which you find yourselves involved, far more by the fault of your forefathers, three centuries ago, than by your own. What I do quarrel with you for is, not your inconsistency in occasionally acting on a true principle, but your adoption, as a general rule, of a false one. You keep the Sunday, and not the Saturday; and you do so rightly; for this was the practice of all Christians when Protestantism began; but you have abandoned other Catholic observances, which were equally universal at that day, preferring the novelties introduced by the men who invented Protestantism to the unvarying tradition of above fifteen hundred years.

"We blame you, not for making Sunday your weekly holiday, instead of Saturday, but for rejecting tradition, which is the only safe and clear rule by which this observance can be justified. In outward act, we do the same as yourselves in this matter; we, too, no longer observe the ancient Sabbath, but Sunday, in its stead; but then there is this important difference between us, that we do not pretend, as you do, to derive our authority for so doing from a *book;* but we derive it from a *living teacher,* and that teacher is the church. Moreover, we believe that not everything which God would have us to know and to do is written in the Bible, but that there is an *unwritten* word of God, which we are bound to believe and obey, just as we believe and obey the Bible itself, according to that saying of the apostle, 'Stand fast, and hold the traditions which you have learned, *whether by word, or by our epistle.*' 2 Thess. 2 : 14. [Douay Bible.]

"We Catholics, then, have precisely the same authority for keeping Sunday holy, instead of Saturday, as we have for every other article of our creed, namely, the authority of 'the church of the living God, the pillar and ground of the truth' (1 Tim. 3 : 15); whereas, you who are Protestants have really no authority for it whatever; for there is no authority for it in the Bible, and you will not allow that there *can be* authority for it anywhere else. Both you and we do, in fact, follow tradition in this matter; but *we* follow it, believing it to be a part of God's word, and the church to be its divinely appointed guardian and interpreter; *you* follow it, denouncing it all the time as a fallible and treacherous guide, which often 'makes the commandment of God of none effect.'"

In another Catholic work, called a "Treatise of Thirty Controversies," we find the following cutting reproof:—

"The word of God commandeth the seventh day to be the Sabbath of our Lord, and to be kept holy; you [Protestants], without any precept of Scripture, change it to the first day of the week, only authorized by our traditions. Divers English Puritans oppose against this point, that the observation of the first day is proved out of Scripture, where it is said, the first day of the week. Acts 20 : 7; 1 Cor. 16 : 2; Rev. 1 : 10. Have they not spun a fair thread in quoting these places? If we should produce no better for purgatory, prayers for the dead, invocation of the saints, and the like, they might have good cause indeed to laugh us to scorn; for where is it written these were Sabbath days in which those meetings were kept? Or where is it ordained that they should be always observed? Or, which is the sum of all, where is it decreed that the observance of the first day should abrogate or abolish the sanctifying of the seventh day, which God commanded everlastingly to be kept holy? Not one of those is expressed in the written word of God."

And finally, W. Lockhart, B. A., of Oxford, in the Toronto (Catholic) *Mirror*, offered the following "challenge" to all the Protestants of Ireland, a challenge as well calculated for this latitude as that. He says :—

"I do, therefore, solemnly challenge the Protestants of Ireland to prove, by plain texts of Scripture, the questions concerning the obligation of the Christian Sabbath, 1. That Christians may work on Saturday, the old seventh day ; 2. That they are bound to keep holy the first day, namely, Sunday ; 3. That they are not bound to keep holy the seventh day also."

In pursuing this subject further, we quote the language of John Gilmary Shea, LL. D., a representative man among Catholics, and an accomplished writer :—

"The Sunday, as a day of the week set apart for the obligatory public worship of Almighty God, to be sanctified by suspension of all servile labor, trade, and worldly avocations, and by exercises of devotion, is purely a creation of the Catholic Church." "Nothing in the New Testament forbids work, travel, trade, amusement, on the first day of the week. There is nothing which implies such a prohibition. The day, as one especially set apart, had no authority but that of the Catholic Church; the laws requiring its observance were passed to enforce decrees of councils of the Catholic Church." "For ages all Christian nations looked to the Catholic Church, and, as we have seen, the various states enforce by law her ordinances as to worship and cessation of labor on Sunday. Protestantism, in discarding the authority of the church, has no good reason for its Sunday theory, and ought, logically, to keep Saturday as the Sabbath, with the Jews and the Seventh Day Baptists. For their present practice, Protestants in general have no authority but that of a church which they disown."—*The American Catholic Quarterly Review*, Jan., 1883.

James Blake, M. D., another Roman Catholic, in a debate with a Protestant, thus drove the latter to the wall :—

"Christ never wrote, but God the Father did. He wrote the ten commandments on the tables of stone, and the only commandment he emphasized was that to keep the seventh day. '*Remember* to keep holy the seventh day;' and there is no command so often repeated throughout the Old Testament. If the Bible alone be the gentleman's rule of faith, he is bound by this commandment; but does he observe it ?—No, he does not. Why, then, does he not observe it ?—*Because the church thought fit to change it.* Here the gentleman admits the authority of the church to be superior to the handwriting of God the Father; and yet he will look you in the face, and declare that the Bible, without church authority, is his rule of faith."—*Review and Herald*, Feb. 27, 1884.

The following statements were made by a Catholic priest in the opera-house in Hartford, Kansas, Feb. 18, 1884, as reported in the Hartford Weekly *Call* of Feb. 22 :—

"Christ gave to the church the power to make laws binding upon the conscience. Show me one sect that claims or possesses the power to do so save the Catholic Church. There is none, and yet all Christendom acknowledges the power of the church to do so, as I will prove to you. For example, the observance of Sunday. How can other denominations keep this day? The Bible commands you to keep the Sabbath day. Sunday is not the Sabbath day; no man dare assert that it is; for the Bible says as plainly as words can make it, that the seventh day is the Sabbath, *i. e.* Saturday; for we know Sunday to be the first day of the week. Besides, the Jews have been keeping the Sabbath day unto the present time. I am not a rich man, but I will give $1,000 to any man who will prove by the Bible alone that Sunday is the day we are bound to keep. No, it cannot be done; it is impossible. The observance of Sunday is solely a law of the Catholic Church, and therefore is not binding upon others. The church changed the Sabbath to Sunday, and all the world bows down and worships upon that day in silent obedience to the mandates of the Catholic Church. Is this not a living miracle—that those who hate us so bitterly obey and acknowledge our power every week, and DO NOT KNOW IT?"

These extracts from Catholic authorities might be much enlarged, but ought to be sufficient to show to any candid person the position taken by that church upon this point. It will be noticed that many of these come from catechisms and other doctrinal works which are officially issued by the Catholic Church itself. There can be no higher evidence of the position of a denomination than its doctrinal books put forth to teach its own people. Thus the papal church acknowledges point-blank that it has dared to change the law of God by "substituting Sunday for Saturday." It puts forth this claim to all the Protestant world as *the highest evidence of its authority.*

CHAPTER XIX.

ADMISSIONS OF SOME PROTESTANTS CONCERNING THE CHANGE OF THE SABBATH.

WE quote a few declarations relative to the change of the Sabbath, from those who are not Catholics,—men who are in no wise interested to say anything which would favor the seventh day, but whom love of truth impels to speak as they do.

N. Summerbell, a noted minister and author in the Christian Church, and once president of Antioch (Ohio) College, says in his "History of the Christians," p. 418 :—

"It [the Roman Catholic Church] has *reversed* the fourth commandment, doing away with the Sabbath of God's word, and instituting Sunday as a holy day."

Alexander Campbell, in a lecture in Bethany College, 1848, said :—

"Was the first day set apart by public authority in the apostolic age?—No. By whom was it set apart, and when?—By Constantine, who lived about the beginning of the fourth century."

The Chicago *Inter Ocean*, answering the questions, Who changed the Sabbath day, and when? and, Is Sunday the first day of the week? says:—

"The change of the day of worship from the Sabbath, or last day of the week, to Sunday, the first day of the week, was done by the early Christians; but the work was so gradual that it is almost impossible to determine when the one left off and the other began. It was not until after the Reformation that the change was confirmed by any legal enactment. In the first ages after Christ it does not appear that the Christians abstained from their regular business upon that day, but they were accustomed to meet early in the day, and indulge in singing and some other religious services. It was not until the beginning of the third century that it became customary for Christians to abstain from their worldly business and occupation on that day."

The *Christian Union* of June 11, 1879, answers the following questions concerning the change of the Sabbath:—

"When, why, and by whom was the day of rest changed from the seventh to the first? Has the Christian Sabbath been observed since the time of the apostles?—*Reader*.

"*Ans.*—The Sabbath was changed from the seventh to the first day of the week, not by any positive authority, but by a gradual process. Christ was in the tomb during the seventh day. He rose upon the first. The Christians naturally observed the first day as a festal day in the early church, and as gradually the Gentile Christians came to be the vast majority of the church, they cared little or nothing about Jewish observances of any kind, abandoned the Jewish Sabbath along with temple services and the like, and thus, by a natural process, the first day of the week came to take its place."

We make these quotations, not for any proof that the seventh day is the Sabbath, but that the reader may see the positions which intelligent persons are taking upon this subject.

The high, puritanical claims concerning the change of the Sabbath by Christ and his apostles, basing it upon the fourth commandment, and seeking to sustain it by the authority of the Bible, are being abandoned by many well-informed persons. They see it cannot be maintained, for to do so they are compelled to place it upon the Catholic ground of "custom and tradition," and the "authority of the church." It will be noticed that the extracts already given in this pamphlet virtually place it there. It was a "gradual process;" it first began as a "festal day;" it grew up by a "natural process;" the "Gentile Christians" "abandoned the Jewish Sabbath" when they "came to be the vast majority of the church;" and so Sunday at last came to be observed as the Sabbath day by the Catholic Church, from whence the whole Protestant world has received it. Well, this expresses as nearly the truth in the matter as we could reasonably expect from the eminent Protestant journal from which these expressions are quoted. It well knows that Sunday has no divine authority for its sanctity; if it had, it would certainly give it. Our readers who have traced this argument through, have found therein plenty of evidence that this "natural process" of the *Christian Union* was never secured until emperors, popes, and councils had used their utmost authority to *force* the Sunday Sabbath upon the people; that men were placed under a curse, and sometimes whipped, fined, and imprisoned, yes, and the Inquisition with its tortures was resorted to, and some were burned at the stake, before the "*natural process*" was fully consummated, and the Sunday of "pope and pagan" fully recognized as a sacred institution.

We have now traced the process of changing the Sabbath from the seventh to the first day of the week, from the apostolic age, when it was ever regarded as merely a secular day; through the second century, when it began to be regarded, with Good Friday and other days, as a "voluntary festival" on which religious meetings were held, and to which some little honor was paid by Christians, seeing that it was generally regarded among their heathen neighbors as a weekly festival day in honor of the sun. In the third century, "custom and tradition," and the efforts of the bishop of Rome and his sympathizers, exalted Sunday still higher, and lowered the Sabbath in public estimation, by turning the latter into a fast and the former into a joyous festival. They had also by this time begun calling it by the honorable title of "Lord's Day," for which there is no warrant in Scripture. The process went on still more rapidly during the fourth century, inasmuch as heathenism and Christianity at this time espoused each other in *un*holy wedlock. Then Constantine, a heathen emperor, issued a heathen decree making the "venerable day of the sun" a rest day by imperial power, which Sylvester, bishop of Rome, cunningly sanctioned and enforced as a Christian institution, by the power of the Catholic Church; and after a season the Catholic Council of Laodicea placed the observance of the true Sabbath under a curse.

With the perseverance of a sleuth-hound following his game, the Roman Church still pursued its work of suppressing the Sabbath during the fifth, sixth, seventh, eighth, and following centuries, and elevating the Sunday in its place, by decrees of councils, curses of popes, crusades of extermination, tortures of the Inquisition, lying miracles, and rolls said to come from heaven, but really originating in the pope's palace. Wherever the papacy had the power, Sunday was established and the Sabbath of the Lord condemned.

When the Reformation arose, its leaders, though men whom God honored by making them a blessing to the world, had through early training so lost the Sabbath from view, and had such a great work of reform on other points to carry through under the greatest difficulties, that many of them did not embrace the Sabbath in their work of reform, though they attributed very little sacredness to Sunday, plainly stating that it stood on a level with such festivals as Easter, Christmas, Good Friday, and other church holidays.

Later, the Presbyterians took the positions held by our Protestant churches generally at the present time,—of trying to place the Sunday under the protecting ægis of the fourth commandment, and of Christ and the apostles,—positions never taught during the previous sixteen hundred years. This late invention to cover a hoary fraud is now very popular with many.

We have seen that various bodies of Christians in different parts of the world not under the domineering influence of the papal see, still continued to keep the ancient Sabbath long after the Catholic Church had changed it ; but that church never neglected, in a single instance, to abolish its observance by persecution wherever it had the power to do so.

We have examined many Catholic authors relative to this change, and they always agree that it was their church which changed the Sabbath. They present this fact as one of the greatest claims of this church to popular regard, and as the highest evidence of its ecclesiastical authority over all Protestant bodies. And intelligent Protestant authorities, with every reason for a bias in favor of Sunday, admit that its introduction was a gradual process, first as a festal day, then gradually coming into favor as a rest day, but with no higher authority than the Catholic Church.

With a brief notice of several texts of Scripture speaking prophetically of this very change, and some general observations, we will close this treatise.

CHAPTER XX.

GENERAL OBSERVATIONS AND CONCLUSIONS.

IN the seventh chapter of Daniel we have one of the most remarkable prophecies of the Bible. It presents a chain of prophecy covering the principal kingdoms of the world for nearly 3,000 years. Babylon, Media and Persia, Grecia, Rome, and the ten kingdoms into which the latter was divided, were presented to the prophet under the symbols of four great monsters coming up out of the sea, —a lion with eagle's wings, a bear with three ribs in its mouth, a leopard with four heads, and a terrible nondescript beast with ten horns, great iron teeth, and a ferocity unprecedented. This last was presented under two phases, corresponding to the two diverse appearances in which Rome presented itself to the world,—Rome ruled by the Cæsars as a heathen power, and Rome ruled by the popes as a professedly Christian power. The latter form was to continue until the fires of the Judgment day should utterly destroy it.

We have not space to enter into a lengthy exposition of this chapter. Suffice it to say that in our application of these symbols mentioned, we agree with the best Protestant expositors; and, indeed, we could not give an intelligent exposition of the chapter without taking their positions.

Verse 23 reads: "Thus he [the angel] said, The fourth beast shall be the fourth kingdom upon earth." Daniel lived in the time of Babylon. The fourth great kingdom from that time could be no other than that of Rome. This power is first presented as a beast with ten horns, and subsequently with three of these "horns plucked up by the roots;" and a "little horn" with "eyes like the eyes of man, and a mouth speaking great things." Then the solemn scene of the great Judgment day is presented, one like the "Ancient of days"—God the Father—sitting with myriads of heavenly angels in attendance. "The Judgment was set, and the books were opened." Then he beheld the body of this beast destroyed in the burning flames of the last day. In the explanation of these symbols given by the angel of God, he informs the prophet that these four beasts are "four kings," or kingdoms, the fourth being Rome. The ten horns he also says are "ten kings," or kingdoms, which are evidently the kingdoms of the Western empire, into which Rome was divided between the years 351 and 483 A. D. These the commentators inform us were the Huns, Ostrogoths, Visigoths, Franks, Vandals, Suevi, Burgundians, Heruli, Anglo-Saxons, and Lombards.

Verses 24, 25: "And another shall rise after them, and he shall be diverse from the first, and he shall subdue three kings. And he shall speak great words against the Most High, and shall wear out the saints of the Most High, and think to change times and laws; and they shall be given into his hand until a time and times and the dividing of time." There is one ruling power in Europe which wears three crowns in one—a triple crown. No traveler who has ever visited Rome will need to be told who that is. Every statue of a pope in that city (and they are many) wears such a crown. How plainly this ruler has distinguished himself as the power which plucked up three kingdoms! Just before A. D. 538, the kingdoms of the Heruli, Vandals, and Ostrogoths, through the influence of the Catholics, were uprooted, and in that year Justinian, emperor of Eastern Rome, ruling in Constantinople, proclaimed the pope head over all the churches. From this point the papacy rapidly increased in power and arrogance, till the mightiest kings of Europe trembled before this political and religious ruler. His power was unique. Nothing in history resembles it. Never ruling a large territory as his peculiar kingdom, he still possessed an authority over the hearts and consciences of men which no mortal ever exercised before. He had "eyes like the eyes of man, and a mouth speaking great things," and a look "more stout than his fellows." Here is strikingly portrayed that far-seeing sagacity and discernment, and ability to grasp the motives of men, which has held so many millions in thralldom never before equaled. The language also indicates those arrogant pretensions and blasphemous claims never surpassed by any other kind of ruler. His look so stout was indeed clearly presented by a power of endurance through many centuries, which has never been equaled by any other.

"He shall speak great words against the Most High." Here are pretensions seen nowhere else. He either calls himself, or is called by his votaries, "Lord God the Pope," "Christ's Vicar or Vicegerent on earth," "A very God on earth," "with power to open and shut heaven at his pleasure," "and ability to forgive sins," "even to grant indulgences."

He "shall wear out the saints of the Most High." Behold the millions of martyrs whose blood has been shed in crusades, in massacres, in horrible dungeons, torn upon rocks, and burned at the stake. This power has caused the death of more people *for conscience' sake* than *all other political powers together which have ever existed on this earth.* Surely this power fulfills the statements of the angel to the prophet. The best-informed Protestant historians have estimated his victims at upwards of fifty million. Kind reader, think of it,—nearly as many people as live in these United States of America to-day, put to death for religious opinion!

He shall "think to change times and laws," or "the times and the law," as it is rendered by many other versions. The late revised version has it "*the law.*" It was not mere human laws to which the angel referred; but *the law* of the Most High, the power against which he was warring. He shall speak "great words against" God, wear "out the saints" of God, and undertake ("think himself able," *Dr. Clarke*) to change the law of God.

"They shall be given into his hand until a time and times and the dividing of time." This can only mean that he shall really seem to have accomplished his purpose of changing the law of God during this period. A *time* is one year (the ancient year of 360 days); *times* (plural), twice as much=720; a dividing of time, half as much=180; making in all 1260 prophetic, or symbolic, days, each day representing a year. Eze. 4 : 6; Num. 14 : 34. He received his power from Justinian, A. D. 538, and retained it until 1798, a period of just 1260 years, when the French Republic captured Rome, carried the pope into France, where he died in exile. The papacy then received a terrible blow, from which it has not yet recovered.

This language plainly implies, even to a certainty, that the law of God would be changed by a blasphemous apostate power. Those who have read the foregoing chapters can hardly fail to see how wonderfully the Roman Catholic power has fulfilled these predictions, by changing the Sabbath of the fourth commandment, and placing the Sunday of "pope and pagan" in its stead.

2 Thess. 2 : 3-8 : "Let no man deceive you by any means ; for that day [the coming of Christ] shall not come, except there come a falling away first, and that man of sin be revealed, the son of perdition ; who opposeth and exalteth himself above all that is called God, or that is worshiped ; so that he as God sitteth in the temple of God, showing himself that he is God. . . . For the mystery of iniquity doth already work ; only he who now letteth [restraineth now, *Revised Version*] will let, until he be taken out of the way. And then shall that Wicked [lawless one, *Revised Version*] be revealed, whom the Lord shall consume with the Spirit of his mouth, and shall destroy with the brightness of his coming."

Here the same blasphemous power is presented which is referred to in the scriptures already considered. He comes to the same end at the great burning day, when Christ comes. There (Dan. 7 : 25) he speaks great words against the Most High, and attempts to change His law ; here he opposes and exalts himself above all that is called God, and sits in the temple, *i. e.* the church, of God, claiming God-like power. He is the "lawless one," *i. e.*, one who places himself above all law,—is amenable to no law. He can do as he pleases.

We know of no other power on earth that claims such prerogatives as the papacy. As we have already seen, the Catholic catechisms and doctrinal books, and eminent authors of that faith, boldly put forth the claim that their church has changed the Sabbath. Indeed, they cite this act as the one above all others which demonstrates their authority, their right to be considered the one infallible church which can command the consciences of men. The fact that the whole religious world follows the practice of the church, with really no other authority for so doing than that of the church, is boldly presented as proof of its power to change the law of God.

Thus we see fulfilled the plain predictions of the Scriptures, that such a power should arise, and should think itself able to change the law of God. And after centuries of effort put forth to accomplish this very object, the power in question stands forth before the world, and boldly claims to have done it. He "exalts himself" in this very way above God himself. Indeed, it seems he could exalt himself above God in *no other way*. He could not ascend into the heavens, and seize the throne of the Highest. He could not grasp the dominion of the universe, command the forces of nature, or keep the vast machinery of creation in orderly motion. But by really succeeding in making millions of professed

Christians, believers in the inspiration of the Bible, accept the memorial of sun-worship in place of the Sabbath of the Lord God, thus seeming to change the law of the Most High, he has indeed "exalted himself" above God, as the apostle declared he would.

There is one question more which we can but briefly notice: Will God permit this power, which was to "think to change" the law of God, to carry through this deception to the very last? or will he bring to light this great iniquity before time closes, so that the truly honest in heart shall understand this work of apostasy before Christ comes? But one answer can reasonably be given to this question: It would be inconsistent and most unreasonable to suppose that God would permit such indignities to be placed upon his law, and never bring to light this work of the man of sin.

There are certain scriptures which plainly indicate that the last and closing work of reformation at the very close of the Christian dispensation, will have reference to this work of apostasy, and the restoration of the law, as God gave it, to its proper position in the affections and service of the true people of God.

The scripture we have already quoted (Dan. 7:25) strongly intimates this. Speaking of the power which should think to change the law and should oppress God's people, it states that they should "be given into his hand *until* a time and times and the dividing of time." This period, embracing 1260 years, commencing in A. D. 538 and closing in 1798, brings us to the "time of the end." The word "until" marks the limit or close of the period during which this power should have supremacy, and the time that the law and people should be given into his hands. Leading Protestant commentators agree that the power predicted here is the papacy, and Catholic authorities themselves claim their church did make a change in the Sabbath from the seventh to the first day of the week. So we conclude that when the 1260 years allotted to that power in which to hold under his control God's law and people, had closed, a change would certainly come. Such a change *did come*, so far as the power to persecute is concerned. All know the Catholic Church has no longer power to persecute as before. Shall we not, then, for the same reason, look for a great movement to restore God's law to its former position? So we must conclude from this language.

In Revelation 12 we find a most striking prophecy of the church of Christ, under the symbol of a woman clothed with the light of the sun, and having on her head a crown of twelve stars, who brought forth a man-child "who was to rule all nations with a rod of iron," etc. The woman fled into the wilderness from the face of a great red dragon with seven heads and ten horns, where she was preserved for a period of 1260 prophetic days (or years) from the face of the serpent. The woman symbolizes the true church, which commentators generally admit. The man-child is our Saviour, who was "caught up unto God, and to his throne." The great red dragon symbolizes the Roman power, which stood before the woman "to devour her child as soon as it was born," in the person of Herod, a Roman governor, who tried to put Jesus to death when he killed all the male children in Bethlehem that were two years old or under.

The reader will notice with peculiar interest the fact that the woman, or true church, was hidden away in the wilderness from this persecuting power precisely the same length of time that the "little horn" of Daniel 7 was to persecute the church of God and seem to change his law. That period commenced A. D. 538, when the last of the three kingdoms was plucked up by the papacy. About the same time the adherents of the true church, as we have seen, no longer remained in union with the Roman Catholic Church; and they were ever after known as heretics. They hid away in retired places, while the apostate power "exalted himself above all that is called God or that is worshiped," in the very "temple," or church, of God himself. Thus Inspiration represents this wonderful period of human history.

"And the dragon was wroth with the woman, and went to make war with the remnant of her seed, which keep the commandments of God, and have the testimony of Jesus Christ." Verse 17. The remnant of the woman's seed can only be the very last portion of the true church; for we all know the *remnant* is what remains at the very last, as a small portion of a web of cloth after the main part is gone, or a few survivors of an army after the greater portion are dead. We are distinctly informed, then, by the words of Inspiration, that the very last portion of the church are to have a peculiar experience, and are to be marked by certain striking characteristics, which will distinguish them from all others. The dragon, "that old serpent, called the Devil, and Satan," will be "wroth" with them. This can only imply that a vindictive spirit of hatred and persecution will be kindled against them. This must come because of certain great truths and reforms, which Satan hates, that are to be accepted and promulgated by the "remnant" church. As he has always done in the past, he will oppress and harass the defenders of these truths in the last great conflict. What distinguishes this "remnant" church?—They "keep the commandments of God, and have the testimony of Jesus Christ." They are not Jews, but Christians. What is it to "keep the commandments of God"? Is it to keep merely a part of them?—"Whosoever shall keep the whole law, and yet offend in one point, he is guilty of all. For he that said [or, that law which said, *margin*], Do not commit adultery, said also, Do not kill. Now if thou commit no adultery, yet if thou kill, thou art become a transgressor of the law." James 2 : 10, 11.

The law of God, embraced in the ten commandments, contains all the principles of moral duty. To keep that law, we must obey every part of it. In suspending our weight upon a chain, we shall as surely fall if one link breaks as if all broke. It is not enough that we keep part of the precepts of God's law; we must obey all. The same God that spoke part, spoke all. All stand upon the same authority. The same reasoning which James' applies to the two commandments, "Thou shalt not commit adultery" and "Thou shalt not kill," applies to the fourth command as well: "Remember the Sabbath day to keep it holy. . . . The seventh day is the Sabbath of the Lord thy God: in it thou shalt not do any work," etc. Keeping Sunday never fulfilled that commandment; for as plain as the sun shining at noonday is the fact that Sunday is not the day which God, in this the only Sabbath law, commands men to observe. Millions have transgressed the fourth commandment honestly, believing they were keeping it. That God mercifully accepted them while they were living up to all the light they had, we will not dispute. So great has been the influence of the "mystery of iniquity" upon the minds of men, that the greater part of the world's inhabitants have been deceived. The Scripture declares that "all the world wondered after the beast [papacy]," and that "all that dwell upon the earth shall worship him." Rev. 13:3, 8.

This work which the great apostasy has wrought has been a most extensive one; but we truly believe that myriads have honestly thought they were doing God service in keeping Sunday. But that fact does not change the wording or intent of the fourth commandment, nor make God authorize men to keep the first day of the week, when he commands them to keep the seventh. We may all feel a deep sense of gratitude that we have a God so merciful that he makes allowance for men's ignorance of his requirements when they live up to all the light he gives them. He said to the Jews: "This is the condemnation, that light is come into the world, and men loved darkness rather than light, because their deeds were evil." John 3:19. "If ye were blind, ye should have no sin ; but now ye say, We see ; therefore your sin remaineth." John 9:41. When men honestly seek to live up to all the light they have, and earnestly desire all the light God has for them, they place themselves where God can save them. When men see their duty and will not do it, then their sins stand against them, and they are under condemnation. So we hope for the salvation of multitudes of those who lived in ages of darkness, those whose lives were truly in accordance with all the light they enjoyed.

But we see a positive statement of Inspiration that the "remnant" of the true church will "*keep the commandments of God.*" This cannot mean that they will keep merely a part of the commandments, or keep them as changed by the papacy ; but that they will keep them *as God originally gave them.* This is a distinguishing feature of the last generation of Christians living on the earth. This will stir the ire of Satan, and they will have misrepresentations and persecutions to meet, and a bitter spirit of opposition to encounter. So the Scripture teaches. We also have a plain reference to this same great movement in Revelation 14:6-16. We cannot give a full exposition of this most important scripture; but those who desire to investigate this and other kindred texts more fully, will find them further expounded in works published by the *Review and Herald*, Battle Creek, Mich., or the Pacific Press, Oakland, Cal., entitled, "The Three Angels' Messages of Rev. 14," or "The Position and Work of the True People of God."

We will express but a few thoughts here concerning this scripture. It presents to our view the proclamation of three symbolic messengers, doubtless symbols of movements of those whom God has specially raised up to give important truths in the last days, to prepare a people for Christ's coming. These must be last-day messages. They are to be most extensively proclaimed to "every nation, and kindred, and tongue, and people."

The first message brings us to the "hour of His judgment," which must denote the preliminary work of judgment which takes places a little before Christ comes. This first proclamation evidently is designed to call special attention to the fact that Christ is soon to come. Such a message has been in process of proclamation for forty years in the past, in the great advent movement especially prominent from 1840-44. It is still being given in every part of the earth.

The second message of warning proclaims the fall of Babylon. There is no great literal city of that name upon the earth. The term must therefore be used as a symbol. The word "Babylon" signifies *confusion* or *mixture*,

—a religious condition where truth and error are mixed together in systems of doctrines partly true and partly false. This must include a large portion of Christendom. The language indicates a state of moral declension in piety and devotion, which will largely prevail throughout the world in the last days; a state of conformity to a worldly standard; a lack of that earnestness among many who have professed the religion of Christ, in comparison to what has been seen in ages past. We think no thoughtful, candid person can deny that we have reached just such a time.

The third message of Revelation 14 reads as follows: "And the third angel followed them, saying with a loud voice, If any man worship the beast and his image, and receive his mark in his forehead, or in his hand, the same shall drink of the wine of the wrath of God, which is poured out without mixture into the cup of his indignation; and he shall be tormented with fire and brimstone in the presence of the holy angels, and in the presence of the Lamb; and the smoke of their torment ascendeth up forever and ever; and they have no rest day nor night, who worship the beast and his image, and whosoever receiveth the mark of his name. Here is the patience of the saints; here are they that *keep the commandments of God, and the faith of Jesus.*"

Whatever may be the reader's views of the meaning of this scripture, if he has any reverence for the word of God he must believe that here is brought to view a most solemn and important work. No other threatening in all the Bible is so fearful as this. Some great issue is here to be brought to bear upon mankind. We cannot question the fact that this is a last-day message,—the very last to be given to the world previous to the time when one "like unto the Son of man" is beheld coming on a white cloud to reap the harvest of the earth. Rev. 14 : 14-16. "The harvest is the end of the world." Matt. 13 : 39. Christ ascended on high from Olivet, and a cloud received him from the sight of his disciples. The shining ones who stood by said, "This same Jesus, which is taken up from you into heaven, shall so come in like manner as ye have seen him go into heaven." Acts 1 : 10, 11. We see the prediction fulfilled in the scripture we are noticing, and we therefore conclude that this third message is a special proclamation of some important truth which is to test the world just before the Saviour comes the second time.

What is the nature of the work indicated in this warning message?—First, it is a threatening against those who worship a power called the "beast;" secondly, it brings to view a people who "keep the commandments of God, and the faith of Jesus." What is this beast power, against which the terrible threatening is pronounced? It is brought to view in the preceding chapter, Rev. 13. The prophet beheld a beast having seven heads and ten horns, rise out of the sea. His body was like that of a leopard, his feet like those of a bear, and his mouth like that of a lion, and "the dragon gave him his power, and his seat, and great authority." He beheld one of his heads wounded to death, but that wound was finally healed. "All the world wondered after the beast," and "there was given unto him a mouth speaking great things and blasphemies; and power was given unto him to continue forty and two months." He had power to make war with the saints and overcome them, and "power was given him over all kindreds, and tongues, and nations." This beast was finally led into captivity.

The explanation of this symbol is very simple. As the great red dragon of the twelfth chapter, with seven heads and ten horns, symbolizes the Roman power in its pagan form, this symbol of a beast made up of parts of a lion, a bear, and a leopard, can only refer to that power which contained within itself the three kingdoms symbolized by these beasts, viz., Babylon, Medo-Persia, and Grecia. Dan. 7. Rome conquered the territory and subjects of these divisions, and absorbed them, so to speak, into itself. Hence its presentation in the symbol as a composite power. Its seven heads represented the seven different forms of government in which Rome presented itself to the world; viz., kingly, consular, triumvirate, decemvirate, dictatorial, imperial, and papal. The ten horns were the ten kingdoms of the Western empire, into which Rome was divided. It held supremacy, as we have seen, 1260 prophetic days, or years, *i. e.* 42 months, reckoning each month, as is usual, at thirty days. Rome ruled by the popes received its power, seat (the city of Rome), and great authority from the preceding symbolical form, the dragon, when Justinian, the imperial ruler located in Constantinople, proclaimed the pope head over all the churches, A. D. 538.

This beast received a "deadly wound" in 1798, just 42 months or 1260 days (prophetic) afterward, when the soldiers of the French Republic removed the *head*, the pope, and carried him into exile, where he died. His government was then destroyed by a republic's being created in its stead. This "deadly wound was healed" when the pope was restored by the allies in 1814.

The pope has spoken blasphemous words against God in the titles he ascribes to himself; he has "overcome" many millions of the saints of God in crusades, by the Inquisition, the stake, the dungeon, and in every way possible. There is no possible way of escaping the conclusion that the leopard beast of Revelation 13 and the little horn of Daniel 7 are identical. Both predictions are wonderfully fulfilled in the papal power.

Now we see the force of the fearful threatening of the third angel of Revelation 14. The time has at last come for God to reckon with this proud, haughty, blasphemous, persecuting, cruel power, which has dared to change his law, to claim divine prerogatives, and to persecute his saints. God did not choose to do this in the Dark Ages, when not one in a hundred could read or write, when one copy of the Bible would cost hundreds of dollars, and when it was almost impossible to find any which the common people could read, very few indeed being written in the language then spoken; but all were hidden in the dead Hebrew, Greek, or Latin tongues. But he has waited till the great researches and discoveries of later times have opened up all the world to mankind; till the earth is one vast network of railroads, and every river, yes, and every ocean, is constantly traversed by the sail or steam-ship; till men talk to each other by means of the telegraph and telephone from country to country and from town to town; till the busy printing-presses have scattered the Bible like leaves of autumn, in two hundred and fifty languages, to every people, race, and tongue; and till nearly every nation can read and write.

Yes, God reserves this great crisis till all can know his word, if they desire to do so. As it was an age of great light when Christ first came, the Augustan age of poets, philosophers, and statesmen, so God has designed that the last great conflict of truth and error shall come in a special age of light and knowledge. In the time of the end, knowledge shall be increased. Dan. 12:4. God is merciful. He will give all who desire to do so a chance to know his will. Then he sends forth this fearful threatening: "If any man worship the beast, . . . he shall drink of the wine of the wrath of God." With an open Bible in every man's hand, God can consistently threaten those who violate his holy law, and follow longer that apostate power which thinks to change it.

We may now ask, What is the position of God's true people? "*Here are they*," says the third angel, "*that keep the commandments of God*, and the faith of Jesus." They keep them as God gave them, and not as an apostate church changed them. And for that work that church is threatened with wrath without mercy. God's people will be distinguished by obedience to him in this crisis, and will not follow another power. It would be absurd to suppose that when Christ comes he will find his people, who are to be translated alive to heaven, following the work of this wicked power, in disobedience to God's law. We cannot, therefore, question the fact that the last great reform, the final conflict between truth and error, will be over the law of Jehovah. This issue is reserved as the last great test.

Would any say the issue is an insignificant one? They cannot truthfully do so. God has ever exalted his law as very sacred. He spoke and wrote it himself. Christ magnified it and made it "honorable." He says, "Till heaven and earth pass, one jot or one tittle shall in nowise pass from the law." In the very last chapter of the Bible, Christ, the Alpha and Omega, declares, "Blessed are they that do his [the Father's] commandments, that they may have right to the tree of life, and may enter in through the gates into the city." Rev. 22:14. The wise man says, "Let us hear the conclusion of the whole matter: Fear God, and keep his commandments; for this is the whole duty of man." Eccl. 12:13. He says again, "He that turneth away his ear from hearing the law, even his prayer shall be abomination." Prov. 28:9.

This law is not abolished by the gospel, for Paul says, some thirty years after the cross of Christ, "Do we then make void the law through faith? God forbid; yea, we establish the law." Rom. 3 : 31. This law is of universal application. "Now we know that what things soever the law saith, it saith to them who are under the law; that every mouth may be stopped, and *all the world* may become guilty before God." Rom. 3 : 19. So we might proceed, and fill page after page with just such quotations, showing the immutability of God's "perfect," "holy, just, and good," "spiritual" law. Such are the expressions everywhere to be found in the blessed Bible concerning this law which the Deity promulgated in thunder tones from Sinai's summit, with a voice that shook the earth.

Oh, no! this great conflict in the last days concerning this law which demands the obedience of every man, the transgression of which is sin, is no small affair. The very foundations of morality and true reverence for God are involved in the conflict. This law will be the main point of the struggle. God's holy Sabbath, given to man at the creation of the world, kept for thousands of years by his people till changed by the man of sin, will have its proper position in the affections of God's people, who will be translated at the coming of Christ.

The light is shining on this subject already most extensively. The reform connected with the Third Angel's Message in the restoration of the Bible Sabbath is extending to all parts of the earth. It is being published already in the leading languages of the world. Printing-offices for its promulgation are to be found in the United States, England, Switzerland, Norway, and Australia. Observers of the true Sabbath are more or less numerous in the United States, Great Britain, France, Switzerland, Germany, Italy, Russia, Norway, Sweden, Denmark, Holland, and Roumania, and in some portions of Africa, South America, the Sandwich Islands, Australia, and New Zealand. Its adherents are being rapidly increased by the extensive circulation of publications, and by the active labors of ministers, missionary workers, colporters, and canvassers in every part of the globe. There has been a wonderful growth of interest in the Sabbath question in all parts of the world very recently. It is becoming a live question; it must and will be heard. We live in an age of investigation, and there is no theological question being agitated to-day more plain or more important than this. Let the good work go on till hoary error is exposed in all its deformity, and precious, blessed truth shines out clearly to all mankind.

CHAPTER XXI.

SUMMARY OF FACTS ABOUT THE SEVENTH DAY OF THE WEEK.

WITH this chapter and the one following we present a brief summary of facts concerning the Sabbath and Sunday, to remind the reader of the points presented in this treatise :—

1. The great God closed his six days of labor in creating the world, by resting on the seventh day of the first week of time, and thus laid the foundation of the Sabbatic institution.

2. The seventh day of the week thus became God's *rest day*, *i. e.* Sabbath day, *Sabbath* meaning *rest*. One day of the week is therefore God's rest day, because he rested upon it, and no other can become such until his act of resting is repeated upon some other day. This no one claims has ever occurred.

3. There are therefore in each week, as the prophet says (Eze. 46 : 1), "six working days," and one rest or "Sabbath day," and that is the seventh day of the week.

4. That original "rest day" of Jehovah, God himself blessed, because that in it he had rested. Gen. 2 : 3. Thus it became a better day than the other days; for what God blesses is made better by that act. Therefore all days are not alike.

5. God also, at the very time when he blessed the seventh day, "*sanctified* it," *i. e.*, "appointed it to a holy or sacred use," for human beings to use as a Sabbath. Gen.

2 : 3. In no other way could this have been done except by informing Adam and Eve, the only living persons, of their duty thus to observe it. Thus the Sabbath was made for man at the beginning of human history, at the creation of the world.

6. The only origin of the weekly cycle is the appointment of the Sabbath. And as this cycle has been known to all ages, the existence of the Sabbath in the earliest times is demonstrated. Gen. 7 : 4 ; 8 : 10, 12 ; 29 : 27.

7. The seventh-day Sabbath is not Jewish, because it originated more than two thousand years before there was a Jew. The word *Jew* is derived from the name *Judah*, one of the sons of Jacob.

8. We have given the clearest evidences from heathen historians of the existence and knowledge of the Sabbath among other ancient nations not descended from Abraham ; and tablets dug up in ancient cities, and a variety of other authorities, clearly prove that it was not derived from the Jewish people.

9. As the Sabbath originated thousands of years before there was a Jew, and was committed to the ancestors of a multitude of other nations besides the one Jewish nation, even *before* they received it ; therefore it would be more fitting to call it the Gentile Sabbath than the Jewish.

10. Inasmuch as God's rest implies the completion of his work of creation, and since he appeals to the fact that he created all things in six days and rested the seventh as the great reason why he commands all

men to observe the Sabbath, therefore we must conclude that the seventh-day Sabbath is God's great *memorial* of his work as creator.

11. All Gentiles owe their existence to God's act of creating, as much as do the Jews; hence, primarily, they are just as much under obligation to observe the *memorial* of it as the Jews are.

12. The reason why God placed this great memorial in the hands of Abraham's seed for a period of time, is the same precisely that led him to place his *law* in their keeping, to give *himself* to them as the God of Israel, to allow his *word* to be written by them, and then brought the Saviour himself through that nation, viz., because all the world except the nation of the Jews had rebelled against him and gone into idolatry. None of these particulars are Jewish in character; all the world is interested in them.

13. As positive proof that the Sabbath did not owe its existence to the proclamation of the law from Sinai, but that God had a law before of which the Sabbath was a part, we cite the account in Exodus 16, where "he proved them whether they would walk in his law or no," more than thirty days before he spoke his law to the people. Ex. 16 : 4, 22-24.

14. The miraculous falling of the manna on the "*six* working days," with a double portion on the sixth day of the week, while none fell on the seventh, and its preservation on the Sabbath, while it became corrupt if left over on other days, continued for forty years,

thus attesting by more than six thousand miracles in the aggregate which day God regarded as the rest day of his people. It forever annihilates the seventh-part-of-time theory, and demonstrates beyond the peradventure of a doubt that God has one particular day of the seven which he desires his people to keep holy.

15. In the most solemn, impressive manner, God proclaimed his law on Mount Sinai, wrote it with his own finger on the imperishable tablets of stone; and in the very midst of the nine moral precepts, which all admit are immutable and of universal obligation, he placed the seventh-day Sabbath, and commanded men to *remember it to keep it holy*, thus showing it was like the other commandments in character and moral obligation, or it would have been placed with the ceremonial precepts.

16. In the fourth commandment no reasonable ground is given from which to claim that it is merely one day in seven and no day in particular which God requires to be kept holy; but it is the *day of God's rest* which he commands us to observe. This is as definite as one's birthday or Independence day, as God rested only on the seventh day of the weekly cycle. Therefore it is utterly impossible to cover the first day of the week with the mantle of that command which requires men to observe the seventh day.

17. All the reasons given in the commandment for the observance of the Sabbath are such as apply to the Gentiles just as much as to the Jews; one needs rest as much as the

other; both need to keep in mind the true God; both need a day of worship; both owe their existence to creation; therefore both should keep its memorial.

18. As the Sabbath is a memorial of the creation, the observance of it by any person is a "sign" that such an one is a worshiper of the true God, the Creator. It ever distinguishes them from idolaters. Had men always observed it, it would have preserved the race from idolatry. Hence the Sabbath is a "sign," or token, between God and his people. Ex. 31:13–17; Eze. 20:20.

19. The fact that God promised the Jews that their city should stand forever if they would always observe the Sabbath (Jer. 17:24, 25), and then, because they did not keep it, he destroyed their city, and sent them into captivity (Neh. 13:18; Eze. 20:13), strongly attests his high regard for it.

20. By the mouth of the prophet Isaiah, in a prophecy referring wholly to the Christian dispensation, God pronounced a great blessing upon all the Gentiles who should keep the Lord's Sabbath holy (Isa. 56:6), thus clearly proving that it was not a Jewish institution, confined to that nation alone.

21. Our Saviour, when he came, kept the Sabbath, with the rest of his Father's commandments. John 15:10. It was his "custom" to use it as a day of religious meetings in which to preach the gospel to the people. Luke 4:16. He stripped off the burdensome traditions the Jews had placed around it, and restored it to its proper position as a day of rest and refreshment, a blessing to mankind;

and he declared himself to be its Lord, its protector (Mark 2:28), and that it was made for the race of man.

22. Christ had the right to call himself the special guardian of the Sabbath, inasmuch as he was the one who created the world (John 1:3; Col. 1:16; Heb. 1:2), and so was a partner in the rest upon the first seventh day in the first week of time, and thus helped to make the Sabbath. Hence we see *why* the seventh-day Sabbath is truly the Lord Jesus Christ's day, in a sense that no other day can be.

23. Christ also taught the present, future, and eternal obligation of all the commandments of the moral law, of which the Sabbath command is a part, solemnly declaring that not a letter or point of a letter should pass from this law till heaven and earth pass away, and that whosoever should break one of the least of these commandments should forfeit heaven by so doing, thus enforcing the authority of the Sabbath in the most forcible manner possible. Matt. 5:17-19.

24. Our Saviour not only imitated his Father in resting himself on the Sabbath during his earthly life, but showed his solicitude that his disciples should observe it after his death, even in times of great national calamities, by teaching them to pray continually for forty years that the time of their flight from Jerusalem, just before its destruction, should not occur on the Sabbath day. Matt. 24:20.

25. After our Saviour's death, the disciples, faithful to his example and instructions,

continued to treat the Sabbath as sacred time. The holy women would not even anoint his body on that day, but "rested upon the Sabbath day according to the commandment" (Luke 23:56), and came upon the first day of the week to do that which they would not do upon the seventh.

26. For some thirty years after Christ's death we have an inspired history of the apostolic church, in which we learn of the exceeding bitterness and hatred of the Jews against the disciples, taking every possible occasion to persecute and destroy them. But in not a single instance is there the slightest hint that they ever found them breaking the Sabbath. This negative argument affords the strongest proof that the disciples continued to observe that day as they always had before.

27. But in addition to this we have the positive statement of scripture that it was Paul's "manner" to use the day for religious worship. Acts 17:2. This is evident when we consider that Inspiration gives an account of some eighty-four different Sabbaths when these religious services were held. Acts 16:13; 17:2; 18:4, 11; 13:14, 44. The last one of these was a distinctively Gentile meeting, held by the special invitation of the Gentiles of Antioch,—a service which nearly the whole population of the city attended.

28. Not only was it the practice of the apostolic church to observe the seventh-day Sabbath, and hold their religious services on that day, but the Holy Spirit has settled the question forever as to which day of the week

in the Christian dispensation is entitled to the sacred name of "*the Sabbath day*," by calling that day the Sabbath after Christ's resurrection which had been such for four thousand years before, and never calling any other day by that title.

29. Inasmuch as all the inspired writers of the New Testament, from St. Matthew, writing during the first decade after the resurrection, to St. John, who penned his Gospel at the very close of the first century of the Christian era, ever call the seventh day the Sabbath when they have occasion to speak of it, and never give the first day of the week that title, it clearly demonstrates that they had never learned of any change during that time, or made any in their practice; for they surely would have called that day the Sabbath which they kept as such.

30. And in the case of St. Paul, the great apostle to the Gentiles, we have his explicit statement that he had "committed nothing against the people, or *customs* of the fathers." Acts 28:17. Hence he must have kept the ancient Sabbath; for all agree that this was one of their customs; and as it is evident that he taught what he practiced himself, inasmuch as he commanded the disciples to follow him as he followed Christ, both he and Christ must have kept that day. Therefore Paul taught the Gentiles to observe the Sabbath. Thus the churches in Thessalonica, Gentile churches, followed the example of the Sabbath-keeping churches of Judea. 1 Thess. 2:14.

31. St. John, the last writer in the Bible, just at the close of the first century of the

Christian dispensation, still recognized the existence of that Sabbath day of which Christ said he was "Lord" (Rev. 1:10), thus demonstrating that all days are not alike, but that the Lord still has a day which he calls his own, just as much as he had four thousand years before that time.

32. We have clearly proven from a variety of first-day historians that this same seventh-day Sabbath was still observed by the mass of Gentile Christians, more or less sacredly, for centuries after the death of Christ, until by the machinations of the Roman Catholic Church it was treated with indignity and contempt. Finally, all who observed it were placed under a curse by the Catholic Council of Laodicea, A. D. 364.

33. We have also learned from history that the true Sabbath continued to be observed by Christians whom the Catholic Church could not control. It denounced them as heretics, persecuted and killed even those who were remote from its influence during all the dark ages of papal supremacy.

34. We have also shown that in the last great reform entered upon by God's people just before Christ comes, *God's ancient Sabbath*, trampled upon for ages by the great apostasy which has thought to "change" God's law, and which has exalted itself "above all that is called God" in the very church or "temple of God," shall once more stand forth in its pristine glory, and be observed by the people of God as the *great memorial of his creative work*.

35. Thus we see that the people whom

Christ will translate at his coming, to reign with him in glory, will agree in practice concerning the seventh-day Sabbath with God the Father, Christ the Son, all the faithful patriarchs and prophets of ancient times, the apostles of the Lord Jesus, the early apostolic church, and all others who take the Bible for their authority and obey the law of God.

36. And finally, the prophet Isaiah, in a glorious view of the new heavens and earth, after all rebellion, sin, and death shall be forever abolished, beholds all the children of God observing the original, ancient Sabbath of the great Jehovah, meeting together every time of its recurrence to worship him for whom that day is the *great memorial.* Isa. 66:22, 23. How, then, can men believe that the day has lost its sacredness and importance?

CHAPTER XXII.

SUMMARY OF FACTS ABOUT THE FIRST DAY OF THE WEEK.

1. GOD commenced his work of creating the world by working on the first day of the first week of time, while he rested on the seventh day of that week; thus distinguishing the first day as a "working day," while he made the seventh a rest day. Can it be wicked to follow the example of the God of heaven, and work on Sunday?

2. Not an instance can be found in the Bible where Sunday was ever observed as a

rest day, or a hint given that its character as a "working day" was ever changed to that of a rest day. Indeed, God in the fourth commandment (Ex. 20:8-11) permits or commands men to work upon it; and the prophet Ezekiel calls it one of the "working days." Eze. 46:1. Can it be a sin to treat it as God expressly permits in his own law?

3. Not a command in all the Bible can be found to observe Sunday as a rest day or a day for religious worship,—no record of its ever being blessed or set apart for any sacred use whatever; no command to break bread upon it; no hint of any change of the Sabbath in any way; nor the slightest proof that the sacredness of the original Sabbath was ever transferred to it.

4. Jesus worked at the carpenter's trade (Mark 6:3) till he was nearly thirty years old. He rested on the Sabbath, and worked six days; hence he performed many a day's work on Sundays. Is our Saviour's example safe to follow?

5. The apostles and early Christians also worked on the first day of the week, and not an instance can be found where they treated it in any other way than as a "working day." Indeed, as no law was ever given in the Bible to observe it as a Sabbath, it cannot be wrong to work upon it. "Where no law is, there is no transgression." Rom. 4:15. "Sin is the transgression of the law." 1 John 3:4. Hence it cannot be sin to do ordinary business on Sunday.

6. There are only nine instances in all the Bible where the first day of the week is men-

tioned: Gen. 1:5; Matt. 28:1; Mark 16:2, 9; Luke 24:1; John 20:1, 19; Acts 20:7; 1 Cor. 16:2. These instances refer to only three different days, the first being the day when God began to create; the next six referring to that first day on which Christ was raised from the dead; while the one in Acts 20 is the last particular day referred to; and the direction concerning the "laying by in store," in 1 Cor. 16:2, does not refer to any one first day, but to a duty to be done on all of them. It is remarkable that in every instance here referred to, the Scripture record gives plain evidence that it was a "working day."

7. The first instance we have already noticed, in which God commenced his work of creating. The day of Christ's resurrection was one of the busiest days of which we have any record in the word of God. The disciples went out with the materials which they had prepared for the anointing of Christ's body, which work they would not do on the day previous. When they did not find him, they spent the time hurrying here and there inquiring of one another concerning the strange occurrences. Two of them walked fifteen miles on that day, out to Emmaus and back, and Christ himself walked much of the way with them. A strange way to observe a Sabbath! As the first Sabbath of a series gives the proper example for all the rest, it is therefore perfectly proper to travel on a journey afoot many miles on the first day of the week. Thus we have the example of Christ and the disciples

for treating the first day as a working day since the resurrection of Christ.

8. So also of the last specific instance in which the first day is mentioned, Acts 20:7. Paul walked nineteen and a half miles from Troas to Assos on the first day of the week. And though there was one religious meeting held in the dark part of that first day, the only case of the kind brought to view in all the Bible, yet the fact of his journeying plainly proves that Paul regarded it simply as a "working day."

9. The recommendation of Paul to the Corinthians,—for every one to "lay by him in store, as God hath prospered him," on the first day of the week,—proves the same thing. This laying by him was "by himself at home," as many versions render it. Their doing this as God *had prospered them* would imply a reckoning of their accounts, a business inconsistent with the sacredness of a Sabbath, but every way consistent with a "working day." How strange that upon such evidences good people should try to change a "working day" into the Sabbath!

10. After the death of the apostles, during the second century, we find some *voluntary* regard being paid to Sunday, with Good Friday and other festival days, for which no command of scripture was ever assigned, and later on, "custom" was quoted as additional evidence. Subsequently some held religious meetings upon it, and finally the Catholic Church favored it, calling it the Lord's day, about A. D. 200. At last Constantine, a heathen, passed a law (A. D. 321) command-

ing a portion of the people to rest from labor on "the venerable day of the sun." This heathen law was the first ever made requiring cessation from labor on Sunday.

11. From various first-day authors we have shown that Sunday was a heathen "memorial" of sun worship, the first form of idolatry; hence the name *Sunday*. It was regarded all through the heathen world as a weekly festival; hence Constantine calls it "the venerable day of the sun." This fact enabled the Catholic Church the more readily to exalt it among the vast body of heathen nominally converted to Christianity.

12. The Roman Catholic Church continued till the Reformation to exalt the Sunday, fining and whipping men who would not keep it, appealing to base frauds and false miracles to sustain it, till its partial observance became general, while the ancient Sabbath was suppressed. Yet it was nearly a thousand years before the first day was called the Sabbath, even by the Catholic Church.

13. In the Protestant Reformation, those who were engaged in it came from the Catholic Church, and brought Sunday along with them, though many of the reformers regarded it simply as a festival day, like the other church festivals.

14. The doctrine of a Sunday Sabbath, as now taught, was never promulgated in its present form, claiming divine authority for the change, and sustaining itself from the fourth commandment, until put forth by Rev. Nicholas Bound in 1595, and hence is an entirely modern doctrine. It has been exten-

sively taught in Great Britain and the United States, but has not been generally adopted on the continent of Europe. It is a doctrine having no foundation whatever in Scripture.

15. The Catholic Church everywhere claims to have changed the Sabbath, and the facts of history abundantly verify the statement. The prophet clearly foretold the change (Dan. 7:25), and the final reform (Rev. 12:17; 14:12), when this heathen "memorial," intrenched by the power of the Catholic Church in the very "temple" or church of God, should be cast aside by the people who prepare for the coming of Christ. These will "keep the commandments of God" as the Father gave them.

Dear reader, on which side of this last conflict will you place yourself? Which of these days will you keep? Will you take God's ancient Sabbath, ever recognized in the Holy Scriptures as his holy day for more than 4,000 years? or will you take the festival of pope and pagan as your day of rest, and still trample under foot the law of the great Jehovah? "Choose you this day whom ye will serve."

THE END.

www.ingramcontent.com/pod-product-compliance
Lightning Source LLC
Chambersburg PA
CBHW031833230426
43669CB00009B/1330